Enhancing Science Learning through Learning Experiences outside School (LEOS)

Enhancing Science Learning through Learning Experiences outside School (LEOS)

How to Learn Better during Visits to Museums, Science Centers, and Science Fieldtrips

By

Sandhya Devi Coll and Richard K. Coll

BRILL SENSE

LEIDEN | BOSTON

Cover illustration: Photograph of *Tāne Mahuta*, by Sandhya Devi Coll and Richard K. Coll.

All chapters in this book have undergone peer review.

The Library of Congress Cataloging-in-Publication Data is available online at http://catalog.loc.gov

ISBN 978-90-04-41175-3 (paperback)
ISBN 978-90-04-39608-1 (hardback)
ISBN 978-90-04-41176-0 (e-book)

Copyright 2019 by Koninklijke Brill NV, Leiden, The Netherlands.
Koninklijke Brill NV incorporates the imprints Brill, Brill Hes & De Graaf, Brill Nijhoff, Brill Rodopi, Brill Sense, Hotei Publishing, mentis Verlag, Verlag Ferdinand Schöningh and Wilhelm Fink Verlag.
All rights reserved. No part of this publication may be reproduced, translated, stored in a retrieval system, or transmitted in any form or by any means, electronic, mechanical, photocopying, recording or otherwise, without prior written permission from the publisher.
Authorization to photocopy items for internal or personal use is granted by Koninklijke Brill NV provided that the appropriate fees are paid directly to The Copyright Clearance Center, 222 Rosewood Drive, Suite 910, Danvers, MA 01923, USA. Fees are subject to change.

This book is printed on acid-free paper and produced in a sustainable manner.

With much love to Sumintra Appana and to the memory of the late Balram Appana, parents of Sandhya Coll, and to the memory of the late Nancy Teresa Coll and Kevin Patrick Coll, parents of Richard Coll. Both authors feel privileged to have parents, who having little access to education themselves, strongly encouraged their children to achieve the highest level of education.

CONTENTS

Foreword *David F. Treagust*	ix
About the Cover	xi
List of Figures and Tables	xiii

Part 1: What Research Has to Tell Teachers about Learning Experiences outside School (LEOS)

Chapter 1: Enhancing Science Learning   3

    Introduction   3
    Educational Context   4
    Research in LEOS   6
    Structure and Organization of the Book   8
    Assumptions and Terms Used in LEOS Writing and Literature   8

Chapter 2: Formal, Informal, Non-Formal Learning & Free-Choice Learning   11

    Introduction   11
    Theories of Learning   11
    Behaviorist Theories of Learning   12
    Constructivism   13
    Social Constructivism   14
    Sociocultural Theories of Learning   14
    Types of Learning   17
    Formal Learning   18
    Non-Formal Learning   20
    Informal Learning   21

Chapter 3: Learning Experiences outside School   25

    Introduction   25
    Ways by Which LEOS May Be Facilitated   26
    Learning Environments and LEOS   29
    LEOS: Implications for School Science   30

Chapter 4: The Learner-Integrated Field Trip Inventory (LIFTI)   33

    Introduction   33
    Learner-Integrated Field Trip Inventory (LIFTI)   34

CONTENTS

Chapter 5: Integrating Formal, Informal and Non-Formal Learning Using the
Digitally-Integrated Fieldtrip Inventory (DIFI)   43

    Introduction   43
    Blended Learning   43
    The Digitally-Integrated Fieldtrip Inventory (DIFI)   47

Part 2: The Practice of Learning Experiences outside School

Chapter 6: Learning Biological Sciences via Learning Experiences
outside School   57

    Introduction   57
    Biological Sciences   58
    Reflections and Conclusions   63

Chapter 7: Learning Chemical Sciences via Learning Experiences
outside School   67

    Introduction   67
    Chemical Sciences   67
    Reflections and Conclusions   76

Chapter 8: Learning Earth & Space Sciences via Learning Experiences
outside School   79

    Introduction   79
    Earth & Space Sciences   79
    Reflections and Conclusions   92

Chapter 9: Learning Physical Sciences via Learning Experiences
outside School   95

    Introduction   95
    Physical Sciences   95
    Reflections and Conclusions   105

Appendix: The New Zealand Curriculum and Science Curriculum   107

Index   111

FOREWORD

The National Association for Research in Science Teaching (NARST) based in the USA currently has 15 research strands, one of which is "Science learning in informal contexts" where the focus for researchers is "learning and teaching in museums, outdoor settings, community programs, communications media and after-school programs." As a longtime member of NARST (since 1976), I can recall when in 2003, John Falk and Lynn Dierking proposed this research strand. At that time, now 15 years ago, for classroom science education researchers like me, this was indeed a new avenue of research, and one that I knew little about. Now this relatively young field of science education research has many proponents, supporters, practitioners and researchers, and there are several specialist teaching and research publications devoted to the likes of Museum Education and Environmental Education. The development of this field of endeavor through the academic contributions of John Falk and Lynn Dierking is described in a very engaging article by Leonie Rennie (2016).

While the focus of many informal contexts tend to be specific like museums or fieldtrips, and often are not directly related to the work of classroom science teachers, this volume by Richard K. Coll and Sandhya Coll is very different in that it brings informal contexts together, under the umbrella term of Learning Experiences outside School (LEOS), that directly involves the role of the science teacher in his or her teaching, and the roles of students in their learning.

This book is inspired by Sandhya Coll's research for her doctoral thesis, which she completed in 2015. Part 1 presents a strong rationale and theoretical background for this extension of science teaching beyond the classroom. 'Beyond the classroom' is an important term, referring to experiences outside school as opposed to outside the classroom which is a more common way for teachers to conduct activities in the school's grounds. Importantly, Part 2 of the book is based on the teaching experiences of the authors who have put these investigations of LEOS into practice. Consequently, readers of this timely volume can be assured that these descriptions for conducting Learning Experiences outside School have been put into practice, and have had successful outcomes for both science teachers and for science learners.

REFERENCES

Coll, S. D. (2015). *Enhancing students' Learning Experiences outside School (LEOS) using digital technologies* (Doctoral dissertation). Curtin University, Perth, Australia. Retrieved from https://espace.curtin.edu.au/handle/20.500.11937/207

FOREWORD

Rennie, L. J. (2016). J. Falk & L. Dierking; Building the field of informal/free-choice science education. *Cultural Studies in Science Education, 11*(1), 127–146.

David F. Treagust
John Curtin Distinguished Professor
School of Education, Curtin University, Perth Australia

ABOUT THE COVER

Tāne Mahuta, an ancient native Kauri tree in New Zealand, was used to analogize between parts of a tree, and the learning model used in this book:

- *Flowers & fruits* represent the learning outcomes.
- *Trunk* represents the teacher.
- *Roots* represent the learning management system.
- *Soil* represents new media literacies.
- *Water* represents forum/blog.
- *Nutrients* represent Wiki.
- *Surroundings* represent learning outside school.
- *Atmosphere* represents the learning environment.

The name *Tāne Mahuta* is a Māori name, meaning 'Lord of the Forest,' seen in Māori legends as the 'separator of heaven and earth.'

The photograph of *Tāne Mahuta* was taken by the authors.

FIGURES AND TABLES

FIGURES

2.1.	Formal, non-formal, and informal learning	19
4.1.	The Learner-Integrated Field Trip Inventory (LIFTI) (Coll et al., 2018a)	35
5.1.	The Digitally-Integrated Fieldtrip Inventory (DIFI)	48
6.1.	Students listening to ISI staff presentation during an LEOS at an ecological reserve	59
6.2.	Students observing a 1000+ year old tree during an LEOS at an ecological reserve	60
7.1.	Details from slide on nanotechnology shown to students visiting the MacDiarmid Institute for Advanced Materials and Nanotechnology (produced by Sereima Raimua, graphic designer, University of South Pacific)	69
7.2.	Task put to students visiting the MacDiarmid Institute for Advanced Materials and Nanotechnology	70
7.3.	Schematic used to illustrate a catalytic converter, used as pre-visit focus before visit to the MacDiarmid Institute for Advanced Materials and Nanotechnology (produced by Sereima Raimua, graphic designer, University of the South Pacific)	72
8.1.	Students using a model to study phases of the Moon	80
8.2.	Students learning about telescopes during visit to the Planetarium	81
8.3.	Schematic illustrating the tilt of the Earth (produced by Sereima Raimua, graphic designer, University of the South Pacific)	82
8.4.	Schematic illustrating the effect the tilt of the Earth has on density of incident rays from the Sun (produced by Sereima Raimua, graphic designer, University of the South Pacific)	83
8.5.	Schematic illustrating the winter/summer solstices and autumnal/vernal equinoxes (produced by Sereima Raimua, graphic designer, University of the South Pacific)	83
9.1.	Schematic showing heat loss from a home (produced by Sereima Raimua, graphic designer, University of the South Pacific)	97
9.2.	Teacher facilitating discussions between students and ISI staff at the show home	100
9.3.	Students working in pairs at the show home	100

FIGURES AND TABLES

TABLES

4.1.	Procedural component of the LIFTI – Checklist for planning out-of-schools visits	36
4.2.	Social component of the LIFTI – Checklist for planning out-of-schools visits	38
4.3.	Cognitive component of the LIFTI – Checklist for planning out-of-schools visits	40
6.1.	Sample achievement standard – Biological Sciences	58
6.2.	Lesson plan for achievement standard in Biological Sciences	60
6.3.	Pre-visit activities for achievement standard in Biological Sciences	62
6.4.	During-visit activities for achievement standard in Biological Sciences	64
6.5.	Post-visit activities for achievement standard in Biological Sciences	65
7.1.	Sample achievement standard – Chemical Sciences	68
7.2.	Lesson plan for achievement standard in Chemical Sciences	70
7.3.	Pre-visit activities for achievement standard in Chemical Sciences	73
7.4.	During-visit activities for achievement standard in Chemical Sciences	75
7.5.	Post-visit activities for achievement standard in Chemical Sciences	76
8.1.	Sample achievement standard – Earth & Space Sciences	80
8.2.	Lesson plan for achievement standard in Earth & Space Sciences	84
8.3.	Pre-visit activities for achievement standard in Earth & Space Sciences	87
8.4.	During-visit activities for achievement standard in Earth & Space Sciences	90
8.5.	Post-visit activities for achievement standard in Earth & Space Sciences	91
9.1.	Sample achievement standard – Physical Sciences	96
9.2.	Lesson plan for achievement standard in Physical Sciences	98
9.3.	Pre-visit activities for achievement standard in Physical Sciences	101
9.4.	During-visit activities for achievement standard in Physical Sciences	103
9.5.	Post-visit activities for achievement standard in Physical Sciences	104

PART 1

WHAT RESEARCH HAS TO TELL TEACHERS ABOUT LEARNING EXPERIENCES OUTSIDE SCHOOL (LEOS)

CHAPTER 1

ENHANCING SCIENCE LEARNING

ABSTRACT

In this chapter different types of learning; formal, non-formal, and informal, all of which have the potential to contribute to the learning of science, are described. Whilst common in schools, evidence in the literature suggests many Learning Experiences outside Schools (LEOS) do not result in quality learning. We can, and should, integrate various forms of learning and LEOS using a learning management system.

INTRODUCTION

The main purpose of this book is to share with practicing teachers some research, which we have found can greatly improve the enjoyment, motivation, and most importantly the learning of science. This research is based on our own experiences, and the benefits our students received from learning science more actively, and specifically when they went outside the confines of the classroom. This gave us pause for thought, and made us interested to see if these fun activities actually resulted in improved learning; we thought they did, but we didn't really know, or didn't have any convincing evidence to prove it did. We were intrigued to see the research literature seemed to be rather ambivalent about this. Everyone seemed to agree students *liked* going outside school, but that this was often more because it was exciting and different from 'boring' classroom teaching. It also seemed to help that the trips, like ours, often went to interesting places like the seashore, science museums and space centers; places many of our students had seldom, if ever, visited. We wanted to change our practice and ensure such trips were based on research, and the research was in turn based on what we know more generally about how to best learn science. The broad question we asked ourselves was; *What approaches might help improve students' learning experiences outside school?* We wondered how these might improve the learning of science.

We immediately struck a classic 'academic' issue; the use of terminology, which often was not intuitive, which had multiple meanings (and sometimes the same term was used to mean different things). This meant it was not immediately clear, how to understand the literature. The most common, and most relevant, terms we found were *informal* and *non-formal learning*, *outdoor learning*, and *free-choice learning*. Here

CHAPTER 1

we decided to use a single term; viz., *Learning Experiences outside School* (LEOS), to cover all trips to a variety of what we call an *Informal Science Institution* (ISI). Through this terminology we can examine, outdoor activities such as fieldtrips, trips to zoos, museums, estuaries, streams and mangrove ecosystems, and so on. In other words, any place we go to for the purpose of learning, that is outside the school. We are here deliberately distinguishing LEOS from learning outside the *classroom*; teachers may take students outside their classroom, but not outside their school. Examples include a garden within the school premises, which might be used to teach horticulture or perhaps aspects of environmental education. The reason for this distinction is related to socio-cultural views of learning (which we discuss more below); the LEOS are in a different socio-cultural learning environment and we have found this is instrumental in improving student learning – we shall also talk more about this later in Chapter 2.

There are some key areas we need to explore first to set the scene, and to provide the background needed to understand LEOS. This also allows us to introduce and define some other terms; such as formal, non-formal and informal learning, and to consider how we can (and why we should) integrate learning using digital technologies to improve the learning of science via LEOS.

Next we provide some context, showing how LEOS fit into schooling, and the broader educational context.

EDUCATIONAL CONTEXT

As a result of widespread education reforms that started in the 1980s, nowadays many science curriculums are based on a learner-centered, often constructivist-based view of learning. So as seen in the curricular in New Zealand, Australia, Thailand, Malaysia and the UK (to name but a few), modern teachers are expected to provide opportunities for a variety of learning experiences in science, including LEOS. A concise description of the New Zealand Curriculum is provided as an appendix, because New Zealand was the context for our work, and the lessons described in Part 2. This use of LEOS is intended to enrich student experiences, motivate them to learn science, encourage life-long learning, and provide exposure to future careers. LEOS thus already forms an important part of extending science-learning experiences in many schools. However, as we shall see to make the most of LEOS, it is important that adequate preparation is done, before, during and after any visits.

As we signaled above, the research in this area suggests that LEOS and fieldtrips have not been particularly effective as a means to improve school-based learning (see, e.g., Rennie & McClafferty, 1996). It seems that LEOS *can* be an effective approach in linking classroom science and popular culture. But it has been reported that there is often lack of teacher preparation, and also teachers generally play a very passive role when visiting ISIs, focusing on things such as managing student behavior rather than actively mediating, encouraging and questioning students' findings. Managing student behavior in any classroom is a challenge, but it seems this is exacerbated because students are often over excited (and unconstrained!) when outside the classroom and school. School off-site visits also are typically controlled by the teacher, and driven to meet *only* certain pre-determined learning outcomes, with little capacity for students to explore topics of personal interest. So despite the enormous potential, there is a real risk, for legitimate reasons related to logistics (safety, behavior management, justification of trips by linking to specific learning outcomes, etc.), that we end up with a learning experience that is less learner-centered in nature. So what we suggest, is that while LEOS are still done to complement classroom learning, where the objectives of the visit are determined by the teachers, it is also important to provide some degree of choice to students. This could include letting them investigate things of personal interest, which are not subsequently assessed.

One of the most important changes needed, is for teachers to structure the LEOS well, and ensure there are strong links between the science concepts taught in school classrooms, and more exciting experiences they engage in when on fieldtrips. As an illustration, the concept of species extinction or endangerment is more vivid and meaningful to students when they are able see for themselves an endangered White Rhino, when visiting a local zoo. It is also important to ensure that out-of-school visits are planned well and used to complement, and not replace, learning activities in the classroom. We will explain this in more detail, and give specific examples, in Part 2.

Although in this book we promote the use of LEOS as a way of enhancing science teaching and learning, enhancing students learning in science is not only about taking learning outside school, but the importance of pre-, during- and post-visit planning. These visits to science centers, museums and zoos (i.e., what we called an *Informal Science Institution* – ISI), also allows for non-formal learning – learning that is not intentional or planned (Coll et al., 2013; Tofield et al., 2003), which complements formal learning. We will explore this more shortly, but teacher planning for such visits often does not appear to draw upon students' prior experience and knowledge, or allow any free-choice learning when visiting ISIs. This doesn't need to become a 'free for all' choice! To illustrate, a teacher can have a formal learning objective related to endangered animals, and allow students to choose a particular animal they can then explore in-depth when they visit a zoo.

What we will argue in this book is that learning using out-of-school experiences can be best achieved by ensuring the learning experience, whilst designed to meet specific curriculum aims and objectives, remains learner centered in nature. This we believe, and our research suggests, can be achieved by integrating formal, non-formal, and informal learning. While there are a number of ways this might be done, here we show how we did this using digital devices, and in particular a Learning Management System (LMS). The one we used was *Moodle*, but teachers can use other LMSs such as *Blackboard*, and adapt our ideas to their own system.

It will be no secret to any modern teacher, that their students use (some would say are obsessed with!) their own digital devices for their social and leisure activities. Such devices are used for playing computer games, using social media such as *Facebook, Twitter, Snapchat,* and various chat rooms to communicate with friends, and many use their digital devices to watch movies and entertainment shows by live streaming. What this means is that activities such as these where communication is 'mediated' by digital technologies are becoming a normal part of students' lives. In our view, it makes sense to draw upon everyday skills, which students have developed from the use of such media, when planning classroom lessons, and also in planning LEOS. Numerous schools in Australia, New Zealand and the UK, already have integrated learning using a learning management system (see https://www.catalyst.net.nz/elearning/moodle-in-schools). While this potentially provides a means for dialogue, discussion, and interactive debate and can lead to social construction of knowledge as part of science learning – as in any learning, the teacher plays a critical role. Not surprisingly, lesson planning with targeted activities and lists of websites to access resources within a safe space are crucial. If construction of knowledge in such social spaces is to be fruitful, teachers need to moderate students posts. This type of interaction between teachers and students, and students and their peers, also serves to reduce what we call *transactional distance* – that is, the apparent 'distance' or isolation some students feel when they are not regularly involved in classroom interactions (i.e., the ones who sit passively and rarely if ever contribute to class discussion). Even the quietest, most submissive of students in class, is often more confident, and therefore more active, in digital social spaces such as Facebook. We can lever off this by making use of digital technologies to foster social interactions between the teacher and students who need and who otherwise may not get individual attention.

Important Points to Remember

- LEOS activities should always include some student choice.
- Make use of students' interest and skills in the use of digital technologies when designing LEOS.
- Learning Management Systems can be used to integrate different types of learning.

RESEARCH IN LEOS

It is interesting and remarkable that despite the potential of LEOS, so little research has been reported in the science education literature which evidences improvements in student learning. It also seems there is very little, if any, inclusion of LEOS in pre-service teacher education programs, although that no doubt varies. Likewise, seldom are there in-service professional development workshops on LEOS, and little is known about how informal learning via a digital medium occurs, and how it might be facilitated. This is especially remarkable, given how focused modern students are on the use of digital devices in their everyday lives, and that the learning environment has changed rapidly and dramatically, with the use of digital media.

Modern students have grown up in the digital age, and most cannot imagine a world without digital media. The use of such digital technologies allows them to access information from home, receive timely feedback from peers and teachers, and feel valued and supported when learning as a community. This suggests that an integrated learning approach may be used as an instructional aide, and help science teachers to construct or implement lesson plans, helping students monitor their ideas, and the processes of conceptual change. If teacher preparedness to adopt innovative ideas, seek professional support, become aware on affordances of *Moodle*, and/or other Learning Management Systems, could allow students to collaborate as a group, this can then help build relationships between both teachers and students who could provide timely feedback and increase autonomy to the silent ones. If this is done, which has been the experience in our own classrooms, increased motivation and encouragement in the e-learning community will lead to collaborative social interactions, which promotes learning, and as a consequence the social construction of knowledge in a learner-centered way.

The education literature says that students can benefit from visits to sites outside school, where science can be both *seen* and *experienced*. However, it seems that most teachers fail to provide proper preparation of their students, and planning of learning activities during LEOS is often rudimentary. It seems that teachers often just use worksheets to keep students busy recording what they observed, and this does not really take advantage of learning opportunities during fieldtrips. Learning during out-of-school visits also is often limited as a result of missed opportunities if the objectives are ill-defined, and if the visit lacks preparedness, and uses poor or no clearly defined pedagogy (Rennie, 2007). Learning under such circumstances may be haphazard, or unintentional. It is important to note that outdoor learning is inherently connected to pedagogies that promote active learning, self-control, real-world experiences, group work and inquiry learning.

Lack of awareness on the importance of informal learning and its potential contribution towards understanding of scientific concepts taught in classrooms, may then mean LEOS will struggle to gain much recognition. But the fact that LEOS are part of the school calendar in many schools, and that each year schools provide resources, staffing and finance to support out-of-school learning experiences. This suggests LEOS is actually already an integral part of science learning – albeit a not well managed one. Students construct knowledge through social interactions and LEOS provides an opportunity where students could collaborate better, which may promote active learning. However, teachers seldom include students in planning for LEOS programs. As a consequence, there are seldom curriculum-related objectives, meaning students tend to 'wander around' the ISI aimlessly, with no clear purpose, and are not able to appreciate the importance of informal learning, and how it influences their understanding of science in their everyday lives.

CHAPTER 1

Important Points to Remember

- There is relatively little research published about learning science through LEOS.
- LEOS seldom involves much pre-visit planning, meaning we often fail to realize the full learning potential of LEOS.

STRUCTURE AND ORGANIZATION OF THE BOOK

This book explores ways of enhancing student learning experiences outside school (LEOS), and we begin by providing a short summary of what the education research literature has to say about how we can best use LEOS to improve the learning of science.

In Part 1, after this introduction, we work through the meaning of the key terms; *Formal, Informal, Non-Formal* and *Free-Choice Learning*. We then talk more about LEOS, and consider how we can integrate these different types of learning approaches using digital technologies. Here, we introduce a model we developed in our research: the *Learner Integrated Fieldtrip Inventory* (LIFTI), used to ensure good planning, and then the *Digitally Integrated Fieldtrip Inventory* (DIFI), which focuses on the learner, and integrates formal, non-formal, and informal learning by digital means

In Part 2, we draw upon the background provided in Part 1, and provide teachers with details of how to utilize this thinking in four important science learning areas: viz., Biological Sciences, Chemical Sciences, Earth & Space Sciences, and Physical Sciences.

ASSUMPTIONS AND TERMS USED IN LEOS WRITING AND LITERATURE

To ensure teachers understand our thinking, we have detailed here the key assumptions, which underpin our thinking, that informed our research, and upon which this book is based.

The following assumptions are central to this book:

1. Individuals construct knowledge during out-of-school visits by participating in activities where they interact with others and with artifacts (e.g., interactive exhibits, signage, etc.).
2. The construction of knowledge is influenced by the learner's context, prior knowledge and social interactions with teachers, ISI staff and other students.
3. Digital space allows students significant autonomy, and this encourages active participation in learning.
4. LEOS helps in conceptual learning, enrichment, social and emotional engagement, improving attitude to science, and reinforcement of certain content.

There are a number of terms used in this area of writing, and so we provide definitions, which are explored in more detail in the next chapters.

Learning Experiences outside School (LEOS)

LEOS refers to visits to a variety of out-of-school environments such as natural history museums, zoos, science centers, planetariums, and visits to manufacturing industries.

Social Constructivism

Social constructivism emphasizes the collaborative nature of learning where students learn through social interactions in the construction of knowledge, either face-to-face or virtually.

Field-based Experiences

Field-based experiences refers to different types of engagement students make during LEOS including engagement with artifacts, ISI staff, other students, teachers, community helpers and parents.

Informal Science Institution (ISI)

ISI refers to a wide variety of institutions or places outsides schools where science may be learned, including but not restricted to, zoos, museums, science centers and the outdoors.

ISI Staff

ISI staff refers to staff who are formally identified as education officers at different ISIs, or who serve in some capacity to help visitors learn about the content and artifacts provided by the ISI.

Moodle

Moodle is an acronym for Modular Object Oriented Dynamic Learning Environment, an open-source e-learning software platform. Moodle is one of several Learning Management Systems, and is widely used in New Zealand, the context for this work.

Formal Learning

Formal learning is structured, intentional learning, that is driven by a school or national curricular. For example, regular lessons about genetics in school.

CHAPTER 1

Non-Formal Learning

Non-formal learning is unintentional learning, which occurs outside formal learning environments. For example, a student voluntarily choosing to attend a summer school exploring a local estuary.

Informal Learning

Informal learning is voluntary learning that is not organized, and is characterized by free choice by the student. For example, a student watches a documentary on National Geographic Channel about poaching of White Rhinos.

Free-Choice Learning

Free-choice learning is learning in which the learner has choice over the content, place or process involved in learning. For example, a student goes to a local zoo with his or her family for a family outing, and reads signage about why White Rhinos are an endangered species.

REFERENCES

Coll, R. K., Gilbert, J. K., Pilot, A., & Streller, S. (2013). How to benefit from informal and interdisciplinary dimension of chemistry in teaching. In I. Eilks & A. Hofstein (Eds.), *Teaching chemistry – A studybook: A practical guide and textbook for student teachers, teacher trainees and teachers* (pp. 241–268). Rotterdam, The Netherlands: Sense Publishers.
Rennie, L. J., & Johnston, D. J. (2007). Research on learning from museum. In J. H. Falk, L. D. Dierking, & S. Foutz (Eds.), *In principle, in practice: Museums as learning institutions* (pp. 57–73). Walnut Creek, CA: Alta Mira Press.
Rennie, L. J., & McClafferty, T. P. (1996). Science centres and science learning. *Studies in Science Education, 27*, 53–98.
Tofield, S., Coll, R. K., Vyle, B., & Bolstad, R. (2003). Zoos as a source of free choice learning. *Research in Science and Technological Education, 21*(1), 67–99.

CHAPTER 2

FORMAL, INFORMAL, NON-FORMAL LEARNING & FREE-CHOICE LEARNING

ABSTRACT

There are different theories of learning, that sit within paradigms, and which represent different world views. In this chapter the most common theories of learning; namely, behaviorism, constructivism, social constructivism, and socio-cultural theories, are described and contextualized, to inform best practice in Learning Experiences outside Schools (LEOS).

INTRODUCTION

We don't want to burden you with too much theory, but we do want to show how our research and classroom practice has been influenced by a robust understanding of contemporary thinking about how students learn best, and in particular how they best learn science. So, we will briefly summarize current thinking about learning, and then use this to further develop our understanding of formal, non-formal and informal learning.

THEORIES OF LEARNING

As most teachers will be aware, the 1980s saw a dramatic shift in our understanding of how people learn, resulting in worldwide curriculum reforms. Modern theories of learning resulted in a shift in thinking from viewing learning as occurring by *transmission*, to learning conceptualized as the *construction* of knowledge, in a particular social context. There are three main theories of learning; behaviorist or traditional, constructivist, and sociocultural theories of learning. Constructivist views of learning have been those most used as a referent for teaching and learning, having a premise that learners do not passively acquire knowledge, but create it in their own minds. As Ausubel (1968) noted, the main thing influencing this knowledge construction is what the learner already knows. It is quite some time ago, Ausubel made this statement, but Ausubel's ideas like those of Vygotsky and Dewey still influence our thinking about the learning process. Such thinking led to teachers trying to *facilitate* students' construction of knowledge, moving away from 'teaching' them via transmission of content. So that is what we mean when we say constructivism served as a 'referent' for modern teaching; we 'refer' to the thinking underpinning

CHAPTER 2

constructivism so as to teach better. It was constructivism that underpinned the curriculum reforms, into what is now quite widespread – viz., a curriculum that strives to be *learner centered* in nature. Social constructivism, which is one of many variants of constructivism, focuses our attention on the *social* processes operating in the classroom by which a teacher can promote a learning community in which students and the teacher 'co-construct' knowledge. Here the original notion of constructivism being the *personal* construction of knowledge in one's own mind, was supplanted by an understanding that almost any learning occurs in a social context (e.g., a school, or an ISI). More recently, sociocultural theories of learning further emphasize the social component of teaching, arguing that learning is an inherently social activity that *always* involves participation in a particular social setting.

BEHAVIORIST THEORIES OF LEARNING

Behaviorist theory was the dominant theory of learning in the first half of the last century (Duit & Treagust, 1995). Behaviorists consider human behavior to be rule-governed, or a response to either an internal or external stimulus. Here learning and teaching is investigated using the methods of the sciences.

Behaviorism is based on a scientific or positivist view of the world. Positivism claims that science provides us with the clearest possible ideal of knowledge, and is based on the assumption of determinism, which means that events have causes and are *determined* by other circumstances, and that science proceeds on the beliefs of these causal links that can be uncovered and understood. The second assumption of positivism is that of *empiricism*. This means that reliable knowledge can only be derived from experience, which provides evidence and yields (preferably empirical) data. The third assumption underlying the work of the scientist is *parsimony*, which consists of providing the most economical (i.e., parsimonious or simple) explanation (e.g., if someone comes into the classroom wet, we assume it is raining, not that they have been swimming in their clothes!). The final assumption of positivism is that of *generality*, which plays an important part in both the deductive and the inductive methods of reasoning. Here observations made are used to generalize their findings to the world at large. This is deemed desirable because positivists are concerned with explanations of human behavior in a general sense. Improving learning within this view of the world is based on changing student and teacher behaviors, and is viewed as the transmission of knowledge from the teacher to the learner, within a reward-based framework. Within a behaviorist view of learning, up to the 1970s, the focus in educational research and our understanding of learning, was based on whether or not teaching practices or curriculum design resulted in changes in student academic performance, rather than how this knowledge was acquired. According to well-known constructivism advocates and researchers such as Reindeers Duit and David Treagust, curricula design based on behaviorist theory were not particularly successful, with Duit and Treagust saying students seldom achieved intended learning outcomes (see, e.g., Duit & Treagust, 1998).

Many years of research suggested that students, even very bright students, had not in fact learned what we wanted them to learn. The *Learning in Science Project* (LISP) (Bell et al., 1990) is arguably the best known, but Duit and colleagues over many years published massive bibliographies of students' 'alternative conceptions,' providing evidence of widespread lack of understanding of fundamental science concepts like force and electricity. This was attributed to traditional modes of teaching with its roots in behaviorism and positivism.[1] So over time there developed considerable dissatisfaction with positivism and behaviorist theories of learning, which in turn led to deeper consideration of how students learn. As alluded to earlier, one conclusion drawn was what the student brought to the classroom greatly influenced their learning. Ausubel and Novak in the 1960s emphasized the importance of student's prior conceptions as an important part of the learning process (see Ausubel, Novak, & Hanesian, 1978; Novak, 1977a, 1977b). Ausubel believed that information is stored hierarchically in the brain; new information is linked to existing knowledge, and all knowledge comes from an individual's sensory experiences. A key to applying these concepts to learning was Ausubel's idea of 'meaningful' learning as compared to 'rote' learning – a characteristic of behaviorism, which he felt was of limited use to the learner. This is summarized in Ausubel's famous quote: "The most important single factor influencing learning is what the learner already knows. Ascertain that, and teach accordingly" (Ausubel, 1968, p. vi).

CONSTRUCTIVISM

Constructivism, as noted above, is a theory of learning concerned with the internal or personal processes associated with learning. While there are many forms of constructivism, a common thread is the metaphor of building or *constructing* structures from preexisting knowledge (Spivey, 1995). The metaphor presents understanding as the building of mental structures, and the term *restructuring* is often used as a synonym for conceptual change. In other words, the receiver of information has to interpret new information, and tries to make sense of it based upon his or her past experiences and understanding. People who subscribe to a constructivist view of learning typically identify with Piaget's (1964) theory that new knowledge is *assimilated* (i.e., accepted into receiver's knowledge framework without much modification), or that new knowledge must be *accommodated* (i.e., the new information and/or existing mental framework need modification to fit together and make sense to the receiver).

So in contrast to positivism, which holds that there is a set *reality* that individuals should try to discover, constructivism claims that reality is in fact known only in a *personal* way that only makes sense to the individual. This represents an important and significant shift in our beliefs about the 'real' world, with a shift from a focus finding the 'truth' to establishing 'viability' – by viability we mean what 'works' or makes sense within the user's or student's own world. However, because an individual learner or student is part of a social world, any viability also must fit into that individual's social context. As a consequence, as we said above, from the 1990s there has been growing attention to the social aspect of learning. There is more emphasis on social interactions and in particular, an emphasis on the role of language and social environment in learning, led to the development of variants of constructivism, particularly social constructivism.

Important Points to Remember

- Behaviorist-based teaching is characterized by transmissive, teacher-dominated instruction.
- Constructivism-based teaching recognizes the importance of a student's prior knowledge which should be elicited before instruction, and used to develop learner-centered pedagogies.

SOCIAL CONSTRUCTIVISM

The importance of social interactions was first noted by Lev Vygotsky, who shared many of Piaget's assumptions about how children learn, but Vygotsky placed greater emphasis on the social context of learning, and this formed the basis of social constructivism (Vygotsky, 1986). He emphasized the critical importance of culture, and the importance of the social context for cognitive development. Vygotsky argued that students can, with the help from adults or other children who are more advanced, master concepts and ideas that they cannot understand on their own.

According to social constructivists, learning in a classroom occurs when the teacher provides appropriate tasks and opportunities for dialogue, and guides students to construct their own knowledge through social discourse involving things such as explanation, negotiation, sharing and evaluation. Not surprisingly, social constructivists see language and culture as fundamental requirements for the construction of knowledge.

According to social constructivists, learning is inextricably related to the social setting (and a key tenant of this book is that this need not be a classroom), where students actively *participate* and create new meanings (Preston & Rooy, 2007). This suggests that students may enjoy learning more when engaged in learning activities where they have some choice and control over their learning. Because student's value autonomy and independence of learning, learning may be easier and more enjoyable in less formal environments such as those in out-of-school settings such as zoos and museums.

SOCIOCULTURAL THEORIES OF LEARNING

Social constructivists believe that an important part of knowledge construction is social interaction, through which we come to a common understanding of knowledge. However, some authors argue that cognition is distributed among individuals, and that knowledge is socially constructed through collaborative efforts to achieve shared objectives. Such authors feel that even social constructivist theories of learning did not pay enough attention to the social component, and this led to the so-called sociocultural theories of learning, which we will now briefly describe.

A sociocultural approach assumes that mental functioning is inherently situated with regard to cultural, historical and institutional contexts (Wertsch & Toma, 1995). A sociocultural perspective views learning as a situated activity occurring through participation, as distributed cognition, and via mediated action. Such jargon is a bit off-putting so let's explore these ideas in turn, using some examples to illustrate what this all means.

The first of these ideas, learning as a *situated activity*, views learning as an activity that occurs or that is 'situated' within a community of practice. Lave (1991, p. 14) defines situated learning as emphasizing "the inherently socially negotiated quality of meaning and the interested, concerned character of the thought and action of persons engaged in activity." She also claims that learning, thinking, and knowing are relations among people engaged in activity, in, with, and arising from the socially and culturally structured world. That is, learning occurs within a social situation from which it cannot be dissociated, and learning can therefore only be understood within the context in which it occurs. The emphasis on social negotiation of meaning highlights the interactional mode of learning in which participants share knowledge and understanding to reach a joint construction of knowledge (Rogoff, 1995). So formal learning occurs (mostly) in schools; there are rules and ways of how teachers and students interact. This would be quite different from how students might learn on a site visit to an ISI, where they might learn by reading a billboard about say endangered animals, and discus the meaning with a fellow student, zoo exhibit officer or parent, and see with their own eyes a vulnerable endangered species like a White Rhino. In summary, the context or situation in which learning occurs is highly influential.

A second view of learning that underpins sociocultural views of learning is *distributed cognition*, where knowledge (or cognition) is distributed across a community of practice. The notion of distributed cognition suggests that learning is seen to involve more than just the person, but the "person-plus" (Perkins, 1997), being the person plus the "surroundings." From this perspective, cognition (and learning) is seen to be located outside individuals' heads, and jointly composed in a system of people and artifacts. What this means is that distributed cognition can include the physical and social resources of the setting that serve as a "vehicle for thought," and what is learned, situated both in the mind of learner and in the "arrangement of the surround" (Perkins, 1997, p. 89). That is construction of meaning is tied to specific contexts and purposes, and that it is important to provide an authentic practice through activity and social interaction for development of understanding. Therefore, students on a site visit to an ISI might learn about safety from a health & safety officer or signage, about animals from discussion from the zoo keeper, read about specific animals on signs near their enclosure (i.e., it is distributed across the different people & the signs). This is very different from what they traditionally experience or expect in classroom learning, where they probably view the teacher or textbook as the source of all knowledge (actually distributed cognition also applies in classroom learning, but is often not recognized as such).

The third notion that contributes to sociocultural views of learning is that human action is *mediated action* with learning mediated by tools and signs (Perkins, 1997). This view draws on the work of Vygotsky (1978), and mediated action considers that human action such as learning is affected by psychological tools and signs (such as language, or technical tools like scientific equipment), which are themselves situated in the social and cultural environment in which they exist. Wertsch (1991) says that one way of investigating sociocultural approaches to how the mind works is through exploring how social language mediates learning (e.g., writing or speaking 'scientifically'), that is specific to the sociocultural context in which learning occurs. So, as an example, there are 'proper' or 'correct' ways to write up a report (viz., using the language 'tool') for a school science laboratory class, specific ways to name animals or other species generically. So unless we know what these tools are, and how to use them, we may be deemed to not understand the science topic we are studying.

Important Points to Remember

- Social constructivism suggests that the teacher seeks to create a classroom environment which draws upon students' prior knowledge in which social interactions are encouraged.
- Sociocultural theories of learning suggest teachers need to place emphasis on social setting and ensure learning occurs in a socially-mediated environment where participants have some control and choice.
- Sociocultural theories of learning suggest that to know and understand science means knowing how to use the tools of science, including language, in a way that is acceptable to the scientific community.
- Learning theories can be used as a referent for teaching, and this helps us understand what influences students' prior conceptions have on teaching and learning.

A constructivist-based model of teaching sees the teacher as a facilitator of learning; a shift from teaching by imposition to teaching by negotiation. While it is important to elicit student's prior knowledge, it is equally important to provide opportunities or affordances in the classroom for social interactions. This suggests the role of student's pre-instructional conceptions is important in learning. It seems that all too often these conceptions are not in accord with science concepts or intended learning outcomes, and are highly resistant to change. How these pre-instructional conceptions can be diagnosed, and how teaching can be designed to take students conceptions into account will likely play key roles in the learning process, and therefore we need new teaching and learning models.

Here we suggest that we need to move away from a singular view of learning characterized as formal learning, and consider other types of learning such as informal and non-formal learning. Let's first distinguish the different types of learning.

TYPES OF LEARNING

Every student who walks into a classroom is different. Some struggle with science and need extra help. Some learn really well when they read the textbook, and others when they listen to a teacher talking or when they work the problems out on their own. And there are some who learn by engaging with experts and visiting an Informal Science Institution (ISI) or an estuary where they could see the 'real thing.' So teachers need to include many ways of learning into a lesson. For example, when teaching ionic compounds, students could take notes, read a few paragraphs, use buttons to simulate how electrons move, use a computer simulation, and practice in pairs and by themselves. Alternatively, teaching about endangered animals, students could visit a zoo where they could read signage and learn about the animal from the zoo keeper. Teachers need to integrate different learning styles into one lesson so that the student who learns best by reading is able to read, and a student who learns best by seeing real objects and moving around isn't left out. One of the ways to achieve this is by learning more about what is non-formal learning, and how could this type of learning be included in lesson planning. Non-formal learning is characterized by its own methods, approaches and fields of action. It can occur in different contexts and in varying types of activities. Formal, non-formal and informal education complements each other and mutually reinforces the lifelong learning process

When learning is caught up in what must be taught (i.e., heavily focused on content, and therefore the delivery of content), we prevent learning from taking on a life of its own and evolving in unexpected (and fun & exciting) ways. If we create an environment in which learning is able to flow and develop in whichever way and direction we desire, we will end up learning more, not only about what it is we need to know, but also about things that interest us.

It seems from the literature that many teachers think the current school curriculum is crowded with information, much of which does not relate to student's daily lives. This suggests we need different ways to motivate and encourage students to continue learning science topics. A learning journey is a journey of discovery, intrigue, knowledge and enjoyment. Therefore, it is important to not only use didactic teaching in the classroom, but a variety of both informal and non-formal approaches to engage the learners to achieve their maximum potential. It is this challenge which sometimes limits teachers from diversifying their teaching approaches, since any deviation from formal learning, needs planning and resources. In saying that, it is important to know first what the three types of learning are, and how could they be used in helping students learn science.

CHAPTER 2

There are three broad types of learning identified in the literature: formal, non-formal and informal. Figure 2.1 summarizes the three types of learning, their characteristics, and provides examples of formal, non-formal and informal learning. Each of these is discussed now in turn.

FORMAL LEARNING

Formal Learning is characterized by being teacher-centered in a highly structured classroom, following a prescribed curriculum, as well as having a strict assessment regime. Formal learning takes place in formal institutions of an educational system like schools, or post-compulsory education systems such as vocational training institutions, polytechnics, institutes of technology, and universities, and is characterized by formal, structured lessons that mostly occur in classrooms. In formal learning contexts such as classrooms, teachers are mainly concerned about conceptual change and/or the learning of new concepts and content. The literature suggests that efforts to teach science in classrooms is characterized by a teacher-dominated classroom, and by rote learning of concepts or facts, copying, and a general lack of understanding. Interestingly, although far more children nowadays study science, research suggests that a great majority do not master more than a small portion of the goals set for them (as mentioned in the previous chapter Duit and co-workers provide bibliographies cataloguing such claims).

This is causing a lot of concern for teachers, parents and governments worldwide, because it suggests traditional school science is failing to engage science students especially those from particular cultural and socioeconomic backgrounds, and argue that decline in student enrolment in science is due to disenchantment with the subject (Mallya et al., 2012). Observations of classroom teaching practices suggest this may be due to the nature of the power relationship that exists between science teacher and student. The science teacher is often trying to tell students about or help them to understand the consensually-agreed scientific world-view. Such an approach can make students feel their views or ideas have no value, and this means that opportunities for meaningful discussion are minimized. Hence, students are rarely involved in the lessons, meaning there is a need to shift away from this normative nature of classroom discourse. According to Duit and Treagust (1998), lack of robust discussion where students feel they are contributing to co-construction of knowledge, makes them feel content is king, and the 'Sage on the Stage' model, tends to reinforce such a view. The problem of didactic science teaching in many countries is exacerbated by an intense regime of summative examination (Coll & Taylor, 2008). The content and style of the national examination tend to be more important determinants of the content and process of teaching than the curriculum.

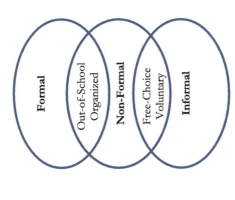

Type	Characteristics		Example
Formal	Compulsory School Attendance	At School Out-of-School	Organized	Regular Lesson at School Class Visit to a Museum Class Visit to University for Project Work
Non-Formal	Voluntary	Out-of-School & Free-Choice	Organized	Optional Summer School Science Classes
Informal	Voluntary	Free-Choice	Not Organized	Watching TV Nature Documentary Family Visit to a Zoo

Figure 2.1. Formal, non-formal, and informal learning

CHAPTER 2

Important Points to Remember

Formal learning is characterized as:

- Being involuntary (i.e., students are required to attend).
- Providing students with very limited choices, if any, of what and when they study.
- Often providing instruction that is by transmissive (didactic) methods.
- Often involving students working alone.
- Involving managed students in groups that are homogeneous in age and attainment.
- Including regular and rigorous assessment of what students have learnt.
- Being under close control of a teacher.

NON-FORMAL LEARNING

Non-formal learning need not be confined to the classroom, and employs a variety of methods for providing instruction and enables choice in learning. It is defined as learning that is voluntary and features affordance for social interactions, which assist in learning. It often involves learning that takes place outside the classroom, such as visits to science centers, museums and zoos. However, introducing resources into the classroom such as TV programs, newspaper reports, inviting guest speakers also are ways for non-formal learning that can supplement traditional classroom practices.

There are a number of aspects of learning that characterize non-formal learning. Non-formal learning is *active*, and often consists of learning by doing. The focus is on doing and assuming responsibility, and not learning theory or communicating via the teaching staff. Non-formal learning is thus characterized by students participating in activities during learning. For example, students demonstrate effects of deforestation or sea level rise predicted by theories of global warming, by performing a drama.

Similarly, non-formal learning is *process-oriented* learning. In non-formal learning, the focus is on the process rather than the content. In this way, the individual path to learning, the acquisition and collection of experience may be equally relevant for the acquisition of skills. Since there is no direct time constraint and no pressure to perform, the methods of non-formal learning can be adapted to the learners, and several paths or different learning programs can be tried out, such as visits to a rock pool and/or aquarium to learn about adaptive features of marine life.

Consistent with social constructivism, non-formal learning comprises *learning as partners*. Non-formal learning relies on active methods of cooperation and on group-dynamic processes. Educating oneself is no lonely, isolated procedure. Self-education occurs in inter-play of students as subjects and their social environment. Students learn both from each other, as well as with each other.

Non-formal learning is characterized by *openness*, which leads to constantly adjusting and re-evaluating one's own set of ideas, and leads generally to a variety of learning practices or activities unlike classroom learning. Students become active co-designers of their own development and learning processes.

Non-formal learning is inherently *learner-centered* in nature. Imparting and appropriating the learning content are dependent on the circumstances. Methods and objectives are geared in non-formal education to the particular participants, and is adapted to their needs and interests. In this, modifications in the sense of setting new priorities cannot only ensue in planning but in the course of learning as well.

Participation, shared responsibility and self-determination are features of non-formal learning. As much as possible, decisions are made jointly with the students, and their involvement in decision-making processes promotes a sense of belonging and commitment.

Non-formal learning is typically *voluntary* in nature. The participation of students in what the out-of-school visit has to offer is not mandated, but the students can freely decide to take advantage of what is offered, or not. This voluntary nature plays an essential role in the youth field since participation here is crucially dependent on the decision of the young people themselves.

For many students, the *Internet* is a source of non-formal information, where they have to filter a huge range of materials available on almost any topic. The digital medium also is used as a social networking medium where students interact with each other, and the learning-varies enormously. Teachers need to take advantage of the prior knowledge students bring to their classroom, as this could be useful component in lesson planning.

Important Points to Remember

Non-formal learning is characterized as:

- Being a voluntary mode of education – the student has the choice to take up what interests him/her.
- Taking place outside the school.
- Allowing time to complete the task – to be flexible.
- Including exams that may or may not be conducted at the end.
- Involving the teacher and taught sharing a relationship of same level.
- Emphasizing self-learning.
- Learning which is done collaboratively.

INFORMAL LEARNING

Informal learning can be considered self-directed learning triggered by an intrinsic drive that continues until all objectives in performance and knowledge have been achieved.

Informal learning can be defined in a number of ways, such as flexible learning or free-choice learning, being entirely voluntary, group learning, occurs outside school (e.g., in zoos or science museums), with a wide choice of learning experiences which could be collaborated using a variety of methods. Learning in places where learning was deemed to be non-sequential, self-paced and voluntary in nature rather than following a set curriculum. *Informal learning is not so much guided by the students' needs, but by their interests.* Informal learning experiences are typically unplanned, casual, implicit, unintentional (or at least not institutionally organized), and thus are always voluntary in nature.

Informal learning is a great outlet for reflective practice or experiential learning. Learners enjoy the autonomy associated with informal learning. They gather knowledge from multiple sources, establish a pattern and choose what to believe and practice. Why is informal learning so popular and easier for learners? It seems it is because of the freedom to explore the degree of knowledge to acquire and the order in which knowledge is gained are all determined by the learner.

From the literature, we also identified a number of other benefits of informal learning, which are now described briefly. Gathering and collecting the desired knowledge is easier today owing to the exhaustive media and devices we have. Informal learning does not require any prior learning experiences or prerequisites. Likewise, learning informally is more relaxing and less threatening for many people. With no exams or projects to complete within limited schedules, many learners commit to learning a new skill or a concept readily.

In an informal setting, students are willing to share more knowledge than ever, and may become leaders in an online community of students where they either post questions or provide answers to questions posted by others. Informal learning is close to natural learning. People tend to follow the pathway that best suits their individual needs. Lifelong learning is a great example of informal learning, and students acquire more knowledge informally than formally.

Resistance to learning new concepts and ideas is also lower when learning is presented informally. Perhaps a better way to approach teaching abstract science ideas is to use informal classroom discussions to help illicit student's prior knowledge, which gives teachers an indication of student's level of understanding. Boredom and procrastination are replaced by excitement and curiosity. Time and cost barriers are often lower in informal learning environments.

Finally, many people recognize that each person prefers different types of learning, styles and techniques. As noted earlier, some students may prefer learning by reading, while others find learning more engaging when they visit an ISI and collaborate with their peers. There is no right mix. Nor does a child learn in one way only. Students can learn in all different contexts, but their learning has to be made engaging and meaningful. Hence, the teacher plays a critical role in creating the learning environment, and sometimes they have to consider different types of learning, namely formal, informal, and non-formal.

Important Points to Remember

Informal learning is characterized as:

- Being entirely voluntary as regards to participation.

- Providing a wide choice of what can be studied, and when.
- Providing instruction in a wide variety of methods, few of which are transmissive.
- Enabling students to work either alone or in groups of their own choosing in terms of age and attainment.
- Only involving assessment, if any, that is of immediate benefit to the student.
- Not being under the close control of anybody with the role of a 'teacher.'

From this discussion of different types of learning, we now look at LEOS and see how LEOS provide a wonderful way of reaping the benefits of formal, non-formal and informal learning. We shall see that well designed LEOS draw upon modern theories of learning, providing an enjoyable and holistic way to help students relate science to their lives, and put the fun back into learning.

NOTE

[1] To download one of these bibliographies see http://archiv.ipn.uni-kiel.de/stcse/

REFERENCES

Bell, B. F., Kirkwood, V. M., & Pearson, J. D. (1990). *Research in Science Education, 20*(1), 31–40. https://doi.org/10.1007/BF02620477

Duit, R., & Treagust, D. F. (1995). Students' conceptions and constructivist teaching approaches. In B. J. Fraser & H. J. Walberg (Eds.), *Improving science education* (pp. 46–69). Chicago, IL: The National Society for the Study of Education.

Duit, R., & Treagust, D. F. (1998). Learning in science: From behaviourism towards social constructivism and beyond. In B. J. Fraser & K. G. Tobin (Eds.), *International handbook of science education* (Vol.1, pp. 3–25). Dordrecht: Kluwer.

Lave, J. (1991). Situated learning in communities of practice. In L. B. Resnick, J. M. Levine, & S. D. Teasley (Eds.), *Shared cognition: Thinking as social practice, perspectives on socially shared cognition* (pp. 63–82). Washington, DC: American Psychological Association.

Mallya, A., Mensah, F. M., Contento, I. R., Koch, P. A., & Barton, A. C. (2012). Extending science beyond the classroom door: Learning from students' experiences with the Choice, Control and Change (C3) curriculum. *Journal of Research in Science Teaching, 49*(2), 244–269.

Perkins, D. N. (1997). Person-plus: A distributed view of thinking and learning. In G. Salomon (Ed.), *Distributed cognitions: Psychological and educational considerations* (pp. 88–110). Cambridge: Cambridge University Press.

Piaget, J. (1964). Cognitive development in children: Piaget development and learning. *Journal of Research in Science Teaching, 2*(3), 176–186.

Preston, C., & Rooy, V. (2007). Planning to teach primary science. In V. Dawson & G. Venville (Eds.), *The art of teaching primary science* (pp. 87–107). Crows Nest: Allen & Unwin.

Rogoff, B. (1995). Observing sociocultural activity on three planes: Participatory appropriation, guided participation and apprenticeship. In J. V. Wertsch, P. D. Rio, & A. Alvarez (Eds.), *Sociocultural studies of mind* (pp. 139–164). Cambridge: Cambridge University Press.

Spivey, N. N. (1995). Written discourse: A constructivist perspective. In L. P. Steffe & J. Gale (Eds.), *Constructivism in education* (pp. 313–330). Hillsdale, NJ: Lawrence Erlbaum.

Taylor, N., Taloga, K., & Ali, S. (2008). Improving primary science education in Fiji by using a multifaceted approach. In R. K. Coll & N. Taylor (Eds.), *Science education in context: An international examination of the influence of context on science curricula development and implementation* (pp. 55–68). Rotterdam, The Netherlands: Sense Publishers.

Vygotsky, L. S. (1978). *Mind in society*. Cambridge, MA: Harvard University Press.

CHAPTER 2

Vygotsky, L. S. (1986). *Thought and language* (A. Kozulin, Trans.). Cambridge, MA: MIT Press.
Wertsch, J. V. (1991). *Voices of the mind*. Cambridge, MA: Harvard University Press.
Wertsch, J. V., & Toma, C. (1995). Discourse and learning in the classroom: A sociocultural approach. In L. P. Steffe & J. Gale (Eds.), *Constructivism in education* (pp. 159–174). Hillsdale, NJ: Lawrence Erlbaum.

CHAPTER 3

LEARNING EXPERIENCES OUTSIDE SCHOOL

ABSTRACT

If learning is to occur during Learning Experiences outside Schools (LEOS), good pre-, during-, and post-visit planning is essential. In this chapter it is argued LEOS should complement, not replace, in-class/school learning, and should integrate formal, informal, and non-formal learning, in order to enhance learning outcomes.

INTRODUCTION

Formal, informal and non-formal learning, outdoor learning, and free-choice learning all are terms we have used in this book to describe out-of-school learning opportunities that are provided at various ISIs. This chapter provides a little more detail about Learning Experiences outside School (LEOS), ways in which LEOS are facilitated, learning environments and LEOS, and the implications of all of this for school science.

Our use of a neutral term like LEOS is deliberate, because it allows us to consider a variety of ISIs, along with other outdoor activities such as the study of estuaries, streams and mangrove ecosystems. As we mentioned earlier, it seems that educational visits and LEOS can bring learning to life by deepening students' understanding of the environment, history and culture, and improving their personal development. Whilst this might be a bridge too far for many schools, (but for an example see the related concept of *Enviro-Schools*[1]), science curricula are seen as the vehicle of instruction for topical issues such as health and environment. Hence, this belief leads to the notion that LEOS could potentially provide opportunities that reflect real life learning processes, something the literature suggest links well with improved learning outcomes in some areas, for example, environmental education (see Dillon, 2012 for more on this).

LEOS may be conducted either locally where students go on fieldtrips, or further afield, such as going on cultural visits overseas. An example of a fieldtrip where children can gain valuable learning experiences is by planting a communal garden. This types of activity allows learning through social construction of knowledge, consistent with social constructivist theories of learning described in Chapter 2. In summary, LEOS are naturally linked to our current understanding of how students learn best; viz., they are often related to everyday life.

CHAPTER 3

There is now some research evidence to indicate LEOS properly conceived, adequately planned, taught well, and effectively followed up, offers students opportunities to develop their understanding and skills in ways that add value to their everyday experiences in the classroom. It also seems that LEOS can have a positive impact on long-term memory due to the exciting, and thereby memorable, nature of their experiences at ISIs. These experiences form a basis for reflection as well as deepening their understanding (Farmer, Knapp, & Benton, 2007). However, it is reported that despite substantial evidence for the value of LEOS, there is often reluctance on the part of teachers and schools to engage in LEOS. This is in part due to concerns such as fear of litigation, cost, or lack of teacher education, and there are a number of reports in the media about 'school trip's going spectacularly wrong.'[2]

A number of reports in the literature say that the value of LEOS lies in allowing and encouraging collaborative learning (e.g., Dillon, 2012; Farmer, Knapp, & Benton, 2007) in a way that is more effective than in classroom settings. It also seems that context is integral to what students learn, and knowledge is a product of the context in which it is learned. What this means is that if school knowledge is to be meaningful to students, there needs to be a link between school science and the real world, and this is something that may be facilitated by providing LEOS.

There are two broad types of LEOS reported in the literature, and they differ in who takes responsibility for facilitating learning. One is where the teacher leads the visit, and essentially runs the show, and the other where the visit is guided and facilitated by ISI staff, such as an education officer or site guide. In both cases, the teacher is still overall responsible for providing learning or curriculum objectives, but in the second case, the teacher takes something of a 'back seat,' handing delivery of learning over to the ISI staff. As we mentioned above, one of the most common objectives given by teachers for LEOS is to increase motivation, interest and attitude which it is hoped results in greater long-term impact than pure factual knowledge/recall that can 'disappear' after a short time. However, as we have seen, if such objectives are to be achieved, teachers need to prepare students for these learning experiences. This is discussed next.

WAYS BY WHICH LEOS MAY BE FACILITATED

There are a number of ways by which LEOS can be facilitated. This includes the diverse roles of teachers ranging from active mediation between the ISI and the school, with planning and monitoring student behavior. ISI staff as well as the nature of these ISIs strongly influences student learning during LEOS. One of the ways strongly recommended in the literature is for teachers to *integrate* visits to ISIs with their teaching programs, and use LEOS to *complement not replace*, learning activities in classroom. The key to deriving the most from LEOS is when learning is facilitated by pre-planning and post-visit activities all linked directly to curriculum objectives, which help give meaning to abstract science ideas studied in the class (Tunnicliff et al., 1997). As an example, when students are introduced to study the topic 'ecology.' It is important that they are introduced to certain terms and definitions *before* the LEOS, and they should be required to report their findings in class upon their return to help enhance their (and their peers) learning of the topic.

Some researchers say that lack of integration of field-based experience with students own prior experiences during planning, may mean students are rarely engaged in small group activities during LEOS (Morag & Tal, 2009; Tal, 2012) – this is where visit planning is crucial. Skillful and thoughtful teachers are sensitive to the learning needs of their students, and adjust their facilitation to maximize the development of independent learning that is self-regulated, personally meaningful and motivated. Such teachers know their students well, and using this knowledge look for personal 'hooks' for learning when planning for LEOS, ensuring constant communication with ISI staff when planning the trip jointly. An example here is when teachers draw upon students experiences and knowledge of local fish breeding conditions and related diseases, when planning for LEOS in marine studies.

The nature of the site to be visited also has a profound effect on student learning during LEOS as mentioned earlier. The ISI should be thoroughly explored by teachers *before* a trip is planned to help facilitate LEOS. It also seems more meaningful learning occurs in some settings because of their intrinsic interest. For example, when visiting zoos, live animals are of more interest to students than signage or presentations from ISI staff (Tofield et al., 2003). A number of studies conducted in nature centers in Australia found that student engagement was limited by the distance they had to travel, the amount of walking involved, having too highly structured learning activities, and fear of animals/creatures that might be dangerous (even if they are not in reality – see Ballantyne & Packer, 2002; Tunnicliffe, Lucas, & Osborne, 1997). In contrast, the same studies also reported that students enjoyed having some choice of what to do during excursion, opportunities to learn outside the classroom, learning together with friends, seeing something new, and being able to actually touch plants and animals.

Teacher modeling also is important in positively influencing students. One way of achieving this is by relating concepts learned during LEOS to students' prior experiences. For example, research conducted in a wild life sanctuary in Belize included a variety of activities such as hiking, night walks, group discussions, all things students liked to do in their personal time (Emmons, 1997; Morag & Tal, 2009; Ratcliffe & Grace, 2003). Similarly, teacher modeling influences the engagement of students during LEOS. As an example, although science enrichment programs housed outside traditional school settings offer unique opportunities to access and use authentic scientific practices, opportunities to be involved in these practices are developed only when science teachers value them (Luehmann & Markowitz, 2007). Teacher modeling is one effective way to encourage students to make most of their time when going on fieldtrips. Take for example, students visiting seashores to study adaptive features of organisms. Teachers during these visits should pick up organisms

CHAPTER 3

from their natural habitat, discuss adaptive features and put them back. This modeling behavior helped ensure continued survival of organisms living in the area.

Unfortunately, with the exception of a few studies that report exemplary work, the literature indicates that most teachers fail to provide proper preparation for their students, and seldom plan meaningful learning activities (Jarvis & Pell, 2005; Oulton, Day, Dillon, & Grace, 2004). Teachers often just use worksheets to keep students busy recording what they observed, and this does not take maximum advantage of the trip. Teacher preparation seemingly ranges from well-defined to undefined plans. However, some teachers are reported to employ informal strategies (e.g., listening to student conversations and probing their thoughts, allowing students to look at information that will not be assessed) to encourage more engagement of leaners at ISIs (Kisiel, 2006a, 2006b). It has been reported that probing students understanding through questioning helped find answers to questions and assisted students to learn collaboratively (Kisiel, 2006a).

It's not all about the teacher, and any perceived shortcomings of teachers! There is also evidence to suggest that besides teacher preparation another factor which helps facilitate LEOS, is ISI staff experience and disposition; both of which can adversely impact on student learning experiences (Coll et al., 2018a, 2018b). This has certainly been our own experience. For example, in one of our case studies, the teacher routinely ran a very active and highly learner-centered classroom. But, on a visit to an ISI, the ISI staff teaching approach was highly didactic in nature (and he was quite resistant to change). The students soon became bored with this departure from their normal learning experiences. This rather undermined the ISI visit, and needed careful management by the teacher on subsequent trips to the same ISI.

In fact, it is quite common for ISI education staff or subject experts to use teacher-dominated approaches, and they typically use lectures, worksheets, over use scientific jargon, and have limited discussions with students. If they ask any questions during their presentations (and they often don't), they typically use simple recall type questions to make inquiries or to clarify student understanding. So whilst ISI staff members reportedly enjoy the challenge of helping students and may be genuinely motivated to help students learn, use of inappropriate pedagogies can impact on student engagement and the depth of learning.

In contrast, well planned activities by ISI staff can have a positive effect on student learning (and again this has been our experience), but only if integrated with pre- and post-visit planning by the teacher. As an example, museum worksheets should be designed to promote and scaffold learning, improve students' on-task behavior and encourage curriculum-related conversations. When this happens, it seems that balancing freedom of choice and scaffolding students learning, results in meaningful learning outcomes. A review of recent research studies in LEOS indicated better attempts by ISI staff to address learning theories in general, and the literature on learning in museums in particular (Mortensen & Smart, 2007; Tal & Morag, 2009). Analysis of task sheets used by experienced ISI staff suggests they are quite different from traditional worksheets, and were designed to promote scaffolding of learning (Achiam & Smart, 2007), as well as increase curriculum conversations that affected students' on-task behavior (Bamberger & Tal, 2007; Morag & Tal, 2009; Mortensen & Smart, 2007; Tran, 2007).

In summary, there are a number of ways of facilitating LEOS. Teacher-led LEOS requires learning to be facilitated by pre-planning and post-visit activities all linked directly to curriculum objectives, which helps give meaning to abstract science ideas studied in the class, as well as choosing ISIs that are more stimulating and engaging. Any LEOS led by ISI staff, should promote and scaffold learning, improve student's on-task behavior and encourage curriculum related conversations by eliciting student prior experiences – to achieve this may require the teacher to guide the ISI staff. It is also important to learn about students' preferred learning environments, which is what we look at next.

LEARNING ENVIRONMENTS AND LEOS

The term 'learning environment' in the education literature has a specific meaning; it refers to the social, physical, psychological and pedagogical context in which learning occurs, and which affects student achievement and attitudes. This is a bit of a mouthful, but Barry Fraser and colleagues from Curtin University in Australia (amongst others) have studied learning environments extensively over many years (see e.g., Fraser, 1998, 2012). These and other studies suggest that student *perceptions* account for a significant variation in learning outcomes, but interestingly this is unrelated to their personal background. This is helpful in that it implies student-learning outcomes can be improved by creating environments conducive to learning. Learning environments strongly influence students' achievement of learning outcomes. It seems learning outcomes are enhanced, if the classroom environment is changed to one that is closer to that *preferred* by students.

Learning environments provided by ISIs such as museums and science centers can contribute greatly to the understanding of science, and encourage students to further their interests outside school. For example, inclusion of topical issues such as health, environment, social and citizenship issues might motivate more students to appreciate the value of science and to consider studying it for longer. As we mentioned above, such sites are intrinsically appealing and exciting for many students compared with a classroom, and there is also the novelty factor associated with going outside school.

Besides learning science in the classroom, LEOS provide diversity in the learning environment in which learning takes place. What is good about this, is that it helps encourage students to see science as a human activity rather than abstract knowledge, and so has the potential of integrating formal learning in the classroom with informal learning that occurs outside school. In other words, consistent with constructivism, science learning may be seen as an everyday activity that can occur in all sorts of different places, not just in a school classroom. The opportunities for science learning beyond the classroom continue to grow in terms of number and

CHAPTER 3

sophistication, and the potential benefits that can accrue. If students enjoy science more through seeing it in a wider context, and develop an appreciation that science is a human activity, they may start seeing science as more relevant and appealing rather than just as an abstract knowledge. Since LEOS are seen to allow active learning, which affects students overall enjoyment and learning outcomes, then it is important to learn about the implications for school science, which we look at next.

LEOS: IMPLICATIONS FOR SCHOOL SCIENCE

LEOS are associated with high levels of motivation, underpinned by attributes of choice about what one wants to find out and to do with, so with a clear sense of purpose. These types of learning opportunities helps develop new ways of thinking, interpreting, analyzing information, which in turn leads to the development of scientific skills. In contrast, the classroom-based curriculum may be limited by less sophisticated resources, constrained by fixed curricula and restrictive teaching strategies. This lack of congruence between students' formal and informal learning environment necessitates the need to explore natural learning processes that operate during LEOS, and the need to relook at the ways science is taught and learnt in schools, not just the adoption of LEOS *alongside* school-based learning.

School science needs to take more account of students' out-of-school science learning experiences, and develop greater consistency to synthesize learning across the formal and informal domains. ISIs typically offer features to guide teachers to develop new teaching strategies, especially strategies that focus on active learning. As an illustration, a science center may have machines or devices which students operate to examine or illustrate, for example, the concept of *force*. But active learning requires a change in both how science teaching is done in classrooms, as well as the role of teachers in facilitating learning. Science learning tasks need to enable rich conversations that extend beyond formal school settings. This involves design and mediation of school-based projects utilizing new literacies, collaboration and creativity, which resonates with student experiences and as noted earlier, LEOS provides us with an opportunity to do this.

Students' informal participation in digital space is altering their social identities, style of learning and patterns of communication. The large-scale availability of the Internet as a learning environment for non-formal and informal learning has changed rapidly and dramatically. The use of digital media for interaction has become, in a short time, a normal daily activity and many students cannot imagine the world without it. The Internet is now used to produce and publish work, critique and analyze important topics where students exchange ideas and learn as a community. These 'social spaces' enable collaboration and conversation among students, where they share ideas with and question each other, the teacher and other experts.

However, central to this type of learning is autonomy and independent learning, which require high levels of support if students are to flourish in intellectually-challenging science learning environments. Further emphasis is placed on the key role of teachers in these collaborative project-based science tasks, in modeling and mentoring to support self-directed processes, especially with students who require learning support. Students need teachers' support to help understand the broader context of their school science experiences, and in developing skills for appraising evidence, recognizing social and other influences and implications for decision making. In Chapters 4 and 5, we provide a model for integrating these learning experiences and environments, and in Part 2 of this book, we take you through some specific examples, providing detailed lesson plans.

While consideration for learning at ISIs such as museum and zoos, digital space, and through science research and display events such as science fairs can help generate high levels of engagement, enjoyment with patterns of deep involvement and commitment, these features are equally capable of failing young students. However, when they succeed, a set of characteristics of participation becomes evident. These include: autonomy, interactions with other peers, artifacts, parental and teacher support, and a creative display of communication in students' social spaces. While these features may not easily be accommodated in school science lessons that involve acquisition of a multitude of prescribed science content, concepts and abstractions, they can provide a platform for building generic capabilities such as new literacies, project management, team work and communication skills.

LEOS are an important part of the educational landscape, and properly facilitated in a given learning environment have the potential to support school science. Visits to ISIs can enhance science learning. Because LEOS can be voluntary and learner driven, they provide opportunities for integrating formal learning in the classroom, and informal learning outside schools, and mediating learning with the use of digital technologies. This could help generate high levels of engagement and enjoyment with patterns of deep involvement and commitment which results in intrinsic rewards from these activities and a deeper level of understanding in science.

Important Points to Remember

- Planning for fieldtrips and LEOS needs to focus on learning, rather than logistics.
- The novelty factor of an ISI is intrinsically appealing to students, and provides more diversity in learning environments.
- Well planned LEOS easily facilitate the integration of formal, informal, and non-formal learning experiences.
- Many ISIs provide a more active learning environment, and facilitate peer interaction, and self-directed learning.

NOTES

[1] For more about *Enviro-Schools*, see http://www.enviroschools.org.nz/
[2] See e.g., http://www.bbc.com/news/uk-england-33634567 and http://www.newshub.co.nz/nznews/new-zealand-mourns-the-elim-school-tragedy-2008041618

REFERENCES

Achiam, M., & Smart, K. (2007). Free-choice worksheets increase students' exposure to curriculum during museum visits. *Journal of Research in Science Teaching, 44*(9), 1389–1414.

Ballantyne, R., & Packer, J. (2002). Nature-based excursions: School students' perceptions of learning in natural environments. *International Research in Geographical and Environmental Education, 11*(3), 218–236.

Bamberger, Y., & Tal, T. (2007). Learning in a personal-context: Levels of choice in a free-choice learning environment in science and natural history museums. *Science Education, 91*(1), 75–95.

Coll, S. D., Coll, R. K., & Treagust, D. F. (2018a). Making the most of out-of-school visits: How does the teacher prepare? Part I: Development of the Learner Integrated Field Trip Inventory (LIFTI). *International Journal of Innovation in Science and Mathematics Education, 26*(4), 1–19.

Coll, S. D., Coll, R. K., & Treagust, D. F. (2018b). Making the most of out-of-school visits: How does the teacher prepare? Part II: Implementation & evaluation of the Learner Integrated Field Trip Inventory (LIFTI). *International Journal of Innovation in Science and Mathematics Education, 26*(4), 20–29.

Dillon, J. (2012). Science, the environment and education beyond the classroom. In B. J. Fraser, K. G. Tobin, & C. J. McRobbie (Eds.), *Second international handbook of science education* (Vol. 2, pp. 1081–1095). Dordrecht, The Netherland: Springer.

Farmer, J., Knapp, D., & Benton, G. M. (2007). An elementary school environmental education field trip: Long-term effects on ecological and environmental knowledge and attitude development. *Journal of Environmental Education, 38*(1), 33–42.

Fraser, B. J. (1998). Science learning environments: Assessments, effects and determinants. In B. J. Fraser & K. G. Tobin (Eds.), *International handbook of science education* (pp. 527–564). Dordrecht: Kluwer.

Fraser, B. J. (2012). Classroom learning environments: Retrospect, context and prospects. In B. F. Fraser, K. G. Tobin, & C. J. McRobbie (Eds.), *Second international handbook of science education* (Vol. 2, pp. 1191–1240). New York, NY: Springer.

Jarvis, T., & Pell, A. (2005). Factors influencing elementary school childrens' attitudes towards science before, during, and after a visit to the UK National Space Centre. *Journal of Research in Science Teaching, 42*(1), 53–83.

Kisiel, J. F. (2006a). An examination of fieldtrip strategies and their implementation within a natural history museum. *Science Education, 90*, 434–452.

Kisiel, J. F. (2006b). More than lions, tigers and bears: Creating meaningful field trip lessons. *Science Activities, 43*(2), 7–10.

Luehmann, A. L., & Markowitz, D. (2007). Science teachers' perceived benefits of an out-of-school enrichment programme: Identity needs and university affordances. *International Journal of Science Education, 29*(9), 1133–1161.

Morag, O., & Tal, T. (2009, April). *Multiple perspectives of out-of-school learning in various institutions.* Paper presented at the annual meeting of the National Association for Research in Science Teaching. Garden Grove, CA.

Mortensen, M. F., & Smart, K. (2007). Free-choice worksheets increase students' exposure to curriculum during museum visit. *Journal of Research in Science Teaching, 44*(9), 1389–1414.

Oulton, C., Day, V., Dillon, J., & Grace, M. (2004). Controversial issues: Teachers attitudes and practices in the context of citizenship education. *Oxford Review of Education, 30*(4), 489–507.

Ratcliffe, M., & Grace, M. (2003). *Science education for citizenship*. Maidenhead: Open University Press.

Tal, R. T. (2012). Out-of-school: Learning experiences, teaching and students' learning. In B. J. Fraser, K. G. Tobin, & C. J. McRobbie (Eds.), *Second international handbook of science education* (Vol. 2, pp. 1109–1122). Dordrecht: Springer.

Tal, R. T., & Morag, O. (2009). Action research as a means for preparing to teach outdoors in an ecological garden. *Journal of Science Teacher Education, 20*(3), 245–262.

Tofield, S., Coll, R. K., Vyle, B., & Bolstad, R. (2003). Zoos as a source of free choice learning. *Research in Science and Technological Education, 21*(1), 67–99.

Tran, L. U. (2007). Teaching science in museums: The pedagogy and goals of museum educators. *Science Education, 91*, 278–297.

Tunnicliffe, S. D., Lucas, A. M., & Osborne, J. (1997). School visits to zoos and museums: A missed educational opportunity? *International Journal of Science Education, 19*(9), 1039–1056.

CHAPTER 4

THE LEARNER-INTEGRATED FIELD TRIP INVENTORY (LIFTI)

ABSTRACT

To integrate formal, non-formal, and informal learning, necessitates a learning model. In this chapter the Learner-Integrated Field Trip Inventory (LIFTI), which provides one way of integrating different types of learning, is presented. The LIFTI comprises Procedural, Social & Cognitive components, all of which must be present in order to maximize the integration of different types of learning.

INTRODUCTION

As we have seen in Chapter 3, if LEOS are to improve the learning of science, they need to be part of an integrated curriculum approach. What that means is we need to carefully plan and integrate all our learning experiences; before the visit, during the visit, and after the visit. There also is benefit when we integrate formal, informal and non-formal learning experiences, because this encourages active learning, peer interaction, and allows students to realize that science learning is not confined to the walls of the classroom. So we need to integrate formal, informal and non-formal learning experiences, and to integrate in-class learning with LEOS. This Chapter deals with the first of these, and explains how to integrate formal, informal and non-formal learning experiences using the *Learner-Integrated Field Trip Inventory* (LIFTI). Given this will involve more work for teachers and costs for the school, the use of LEOS needs to be weighed carefully. Almost everyone has childhood memories of school field trips. Boarding a school bus with classmates for a trip to a museum, play, or other out-of-school activity always made for a special day. Students and teachers alike look forward to these educational outings all year long. It is a chance to get out of a daily structured routine and teaching strategies, as well as a wonderful opportunity for students to make curriculum connections outside of the classroom, that relate to what they are learning inside the classroom to the wider community in which they live. As noted in the previous chapters, in order to maximize learning outcome from out-of-school visits, it is important that teachers conduct pre-, during and post-visit preparations.

CHAPTER 4

LEARNER-INTEGRATED FIELD TRIP INVENTORY (LIFTI)

In recent published work, we described a model, which we have used with teachers when preparing for out-of-school visits (Coll et al., 2018a, 2018b). The model is the *Learner-Integrated Field Trip Inventory* (LIFTI). As can be seen from Figure 4.1, the LIFTI has three components; *Procedural, Social* and *Cognitive,* and these will now be described in turn. Each component is illustrated by a number of descriptors, which can be used when planning for out-of-school visits.

The *Procedural* component, as the name implies focuses on the logistics of the LEOS. Here, it is noted objectives of the visit should be strongly linked with content learned in the classroom (something many teachers already do). However, to ensure this works, a visit to the Informal Science Institution (ISI) before the trip is crucial, in order to understand the learning opportunities available, and to inform ISI staff about the objectives of the fieldtrip, and types of interactive experiences teachers wish to have during the visit. This visit also will help identify physical layout of the ISI, and allows teachers to collect any available information/resource packs provided by the ISI.

The *Social* component focuses on fostering social interaction, and it is our experience that it is helpful if students are grouped with individuals they like to study with; but teachers will know their own students best and should exercise judgment when grouping students. Students' ideas should be drawn when preparing worksheets, but some free choice/informal learning encourages active participation, allowing students to make their own personal inquires with ISI staff. Such opportunities keep them motivated and result in deeper learning (Rennie, 2007).

The *Cognitive* component focuses on learning; something necessary if the trip is to be more than simply a fun activity or reward. Well-designed LEOS can have a positive impact on long-term memory due to the memorable nature of the experiences at ISIs, forming a basis for reflection as well as deepening student understanding (Farmer, Knapp, & Benton, 2007; Whittington, 2006). Hence, it is important to provide adequate pre-visit preparation where students are shown the link between what is taught in the classroom, and the purpose of the fieldtrip. Equally important is the need to consolidate findings from visiting the ISI. This can be achieved by having students present their findings to their classmates, or evaluating understanding by means of a simple test.

As reported in earlier chapters, ISIs have real potential for informal learning, when student learning is self-paced and self-directed. According to Griffin and Symington (1997), the following factors enhance student learning at ISIs:

- Dealing with things/ideas that are real, important and relevant to students.
- Manipulating and exploring real things and phenomena.
- Dealing with ideas that have meaning for students.
- Students working with others, talking and sharing ideas.
- Students participating in learning based on real experiences.

THE LEARNER-INTEGRATED FIELD TRIP INVENTORY (LIFTI)

- Students working *with* the teacher and not *for* the teacher.
- Giving students opportunities to take ownership of what and how they are learning; and finding their own real answers.

It has been reported in the literature that there is a need to integrate LEOS with teaching programs, and use out-of-school activities to complement, not replace, learning activities in classroom (Falk & Dierking, 2012). If this is done, intrinsic motivation seems to be heightened, and deeper learning is more likely to occur when visiting ISIs (Campbell & Tytler, 2007; Dierking, Falk, Rennie, Anderson, & Ellenbogen, 2003; Falk, 2006).

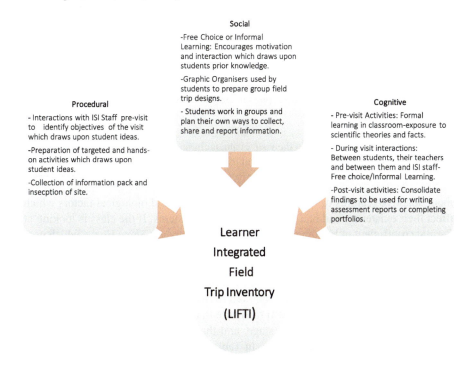

Figure 4.1. The Learner-Integrated Field Trip Inventory (LIFTI) (Coll et al., 2018a)

Procedural Component of the LIFTI

First, are provided suggestions on what teachers need to do before the fieldtrip; these together form the *Procedural* component of the LIFTI. Not surprisingly, the first step in planning a field trip is to find a suitable place to visit! Teachers need to think about what their students are learning, and try to connect an outside classroom adventure that relates to that. For example, if the class is studying biodiversity, then a fieldtrip to a local zoo or conservation park makes sense. Students can learn

CHAPTER 4

Table 4.1. Procedural component of the LIFTI – Checklist for planning out-of-school visits

Procedural		
ISI Staff Besides teacher preparation, other factors which help facilitate out-of-school visits are, ISI staff experience, attitude to help students as well as targeted interactive activities conducted at the ISI which are related to the objectives of the visit (Tal & Morag, 2007).	*Advance Organizers* Packet of information which provides students, and teachers with a map of the ISI, description, *and* a directory of the exhibits. It includes routes students could take around the ISI.	*Work Sheet* Worksheets could be used to provide guidance during the visit, but should be constructed by drawing upon students ideas about the topic. The quiet students should be assigned roles according to their choice to feel more involved in fieldtrip design.

Planning Procedure:
Teachers will use this space for planning procedural component of the fieldtrip. The planning should include all three descriptors namely ISI Staff, Advance Organisers and Worksheet.

Reflection:
Teachers will provide feedback on the visit, evaluate findings by using student feedback, and suggest changes when planning their next trip.

about adaptive features of organisms, habitat, physical and biological factors which affect their existence, and human influence on ecosystems. If the class is looking at thermal co-efficient of building materials, a trip to a modern *Show Home*, which uses contemporary energy-efficient building materials and designs, would work well.

Once the ISI is chosen, the next step is to contact ISI staff to find the dates and times they are open, and how much the fieldtrip will cost per student (if anything). Then all request forms should be submitted to the school's main office, and formal approval sought. It is important also to ensure that an information packet about the ISI is provided to students at this stage, and that the ISI staff are informed about the objectives of the visit in advance. In Table 4.1 we show some of the factors to consider when planning for this component of the LIFTI; viz., pre-, during- and post-visit to an ISI. Teachers need to conduct a site inspection to ensure the site is safe to visit. It is helpful to produce *Advance Organizers* (examples are provided in the chapters in Part 2) from the ISI to plan how to conduct different activities at the ISI. Visiting the ISI provides opportunities to discuss objectives of the trip with ISI staff. It also can help make sure ISI staff organize interactive activities, which are targeted to the topic under study. This will ensure students link the work learned in the classroom with the information collected at the ISI.

Worksheets can be useful during out-of-school visits. They provide a conduit between what is taught in the classroom, and the information to be collected at the ISI. For example, when visiting a fresh water lake to study living organisms, teachers could ask students to select organisms they wish to study (i.e., giving them some free choice), interview their parents and/or conduct a library or internet research on its ecological niche, human influence on population number, effects of introducing a predator/parasite to regulate diversity of other species. Our experience suggests that allowing students some free-choice learning encourages them to get more actively involved. In one of our fieldtrips, parents of some students, who were dairy farmers, displayed a deep understanding of breeding seasons of some aquatic life, and parasites, which affected them. This interaction with parents/guardians and elders is useful because it allows students to get information from more than just their school libraries/the internet, and helps them understand that even their parents/guardians and elders know some science!

Social Component of the LIFTI

Once the fieldtrip has been approved, secure the destination and get parental/guardian consent. This is typically done by sending a consent letter to parents/guardians about 1–2 weeks before the trip. In the letter, be sure to ask for any volunteers to help with supervision for the fieldtrip. Each class needs to have an adequate number of adult supervisors; we usually have about 5 students per adult. If students conduct informal discussions about their fieldtrip with parents before the consent letters are sent home which requests supervisors, parents will more likely be keen to accompany their children. In one of our LEOS trips, we conducted a bird study at the *Tiritiri Matangi Bird Sanctuary*, off Auckland harbor in New Zealand. This was a great success, and a large number of parents/guardians and elders accompanied the students. The accompanying adults were highly entertained, intrigued by how active their children were, and the elders added real value, drawing on profound knowledge about changing population of birdlife with an increase in industrialization and human life in Auckland.

Once you have identified adult supervisors, create a list of duties and expectations that you can give to them on the day of the fieldtrip. For example, make each supervisor responsible for no more than 5 children, and give them a list of names of these children, assigned responsibilities and tasks to be completed by the students. Make sure the supervisors are aware of any allergies or other health conditions the students may have.

It is particularly important to discuss fieldtrip behavior/etiquette and set rules before the visit. Teach and model appropriate behavior, and specify clearly the consequences of misbehavior. If a student breaks a rule, make sure you enforce any consequences that you have signaled in advance. As an example, in our schools we made them lose 'House Points' (i.e., an in-school competition rewards system). Discuss behavior expected on the transportation you use, including things such as where should they sit. Talk about where they will be eating lunch if that is part of the trip, and the rules for that, as well as how to conduct themselves during the fieldtrip. Emphasize that they are representing their school when they are out-of-school, and

CHAPTER 4

Table 4.2. Social component of the LIFTI – Checklist for planning out-of-school visits

Social		
Student Groups	*Control of Visit*	*Control of Learning*
Students expect to have fun which often at the same time acts as a stimulus for more detailed learning (Rennie, 2007). Students grouped with their friends taking into consideration how well they interact and their ability to work well together. If students do not like their groups, they are less likely to interact and experience significant discussions. Students learn by sharing information.	Informal learning, which includes free choice, allows students to take control of their learning. They choose a plan of how they wish to work, with whom and the inquiries they wish to make using advance organisers.	Students enjoy learning and engaging in socially mediated learning environments where they have both *choice* and *control* of what they are doing (Bamberger & Tal, 2007). While students visit ISIs to collect information in order to complete their internal assessment projects, they should be provided with a directory of what they could see and/or do. Students should be allowed to choose what they want to study and explore their individual interests.

Planning Social Collaborations:
Teachers use this space for planning social component of the fieldtrip. The planning should include all three descriptors namely student group, control of visit, and control of learning.

Reflection:
Teachers provide feedback on the visit, evaluate findings by using student feedback, and suggest changes when planning the next trip.

they need to be on their best behavior. It is important to make them stick to the rules, and enforce any consequences that you went over before the fieldtrip. These rules should also be shared with supervisors.

Before the fieldtrip, plan a learning activity. This should be done in the classroom, and should include activities, which should be conducted before the trip, during the trip, and after the trip. Worksheets can be useful documents to provide guidelines as well as collect information when visiting an ISI (examples are provided in Part 2). While worksheets are generally prepared by teachers, it is important to draw upon student ideas, to give them some control of their learning. As we keep saying, some informal or free-choice learning can encourage students to become more actively engaged when preparing for out-of-school visits. An example here is interactional exhibits in museums allow fun learning to occur and act as stimulus for later and more detailed learning (Rennie, 2007). It seems that students viewed their learning at ISIs as entwined with the social environment, and studying in small groups provides an optimal context for sharing information and finding answers to complex issues (Falk & Dierking, 2000; Paris, 1997). By allowing them some control of the visit, gives students the opportunity to prepare their own questions they wish to explore at the ISI. These need not be assessed, but such inquiries allow students to develop ownership of learning, which encourages more engagement. Often teachers group their students for activities including LEOS, but there is merit in allowing students to select their group. If you allow this, ensure the final group is mixed ability (see *Social* Component Table 4.2). Once groups are established, the students should be asked to assign different roles to the individuals they think will be able to carry out these responsibilities. Make sure that students are comfortable within their groups, and that they are assigned different responsibilities. Quiet students can be put in charge of designing worksheets, recording information and taking photographs at the ISI. They can also be asked to assist their peers when presenting findings post-visit, to help them express themselves a little more.

Cognitive Component of the LIFTI

It is important to discuss the purpose of the fieldtrip, and make sure students see how it relates to the topic of study. This makes it clear to the students that they are being taken outside their school for the purpose of *learning*, reducing the likelihood they see the trip as a pure reward/fun activity.

Planning should include all activities, pre-, during, and post-visit. For example, during pre-visit preparation if students are taught about polymer chemistry in the classroom, they can first be taught about addition reactions, and shown how monomers are added together to form a polymer. It is difficult to conduct such experiments in most classrooms (although the production of Nylon does work well: see https://www.youtube.com/watch?v=NQpTQFGKRN8), but models can be used to show how extra bonds in an unsaturated compound breaks to form new bonds, molecules get added together, and a new compound is formed, and so on. While interactive learning using models in the classroom during pre-visit preparation can provide fundamental knowledge on the process of polymerization, a visit to an ISI such as local plastics factory adds real value. During one of our visits, the students were given the opportunity to see actual resin (i.e., the monomer). These resins were then put through furnaces under at specific conditions of temperature and pressure, where they melted and were drawn into plastic sheets. The engineers at the ISI site provided an overview of the process, and students were able to develop a deeper understanding of polymers when they observed chemical changes and saw new products formed. Many products were related to everyday life. For example, wrappers for potato crisps, something dear to many students! During our visit to the plastics factory, it was interesting to note that not only did students ask more questions about how changing the conditions of the process could affect the quality or type of plastic produced, but some were also interested to learn more about the machinery, maintenance, repair and cost of operation. One student asked about the yield per day, and how this related to costs involved in running the plant – deeply impressing the ISI staff.

CHAPTER 4

Table 4.3. Cognitive component of the LIFTI – Checklist for planning out-of-school visits

Cognitive		
Pre-visit Activities Classroom activities completed prior to the visit should be directly related to the visits learning goals. Moreover, the pre-visit activities that are completed in the classroom should convey a strong correlation between the during-visit and the post-visit tasks. These need to provide exposure to a range of scientific theories, models and discussions about the concepts being studied (Goodrum, 2007).	*During-visit Activities* The activities completed during the visit should be directly related to the pre-visit activities. Students can explore questions which they had put together from their group discussions pre-visit, and use this to make inquiries with the ISI staff. Some degree of freedom of choice is reported to have better learning outcomes (Falk & Dierking, 2000). Students have the advantage of exploring topics of their own choice, which are not assessed.	*Post-visit Activities* Classroom activities are used to consolidate learning, which occurred during out-of-school visit (Tal, 2012). The post-visit activities provide students with an understanding of how the out-of-school visit relates to their classroom learning and subsequently findings should be used to complete assessment tasks, either a portfolio or a written test.

Planning Cognitive Collaborations:
Teachers use this space for planning cognitive component of the fieldtrip. The planning should include all three descriptors namely pre-visit, during-visit and post-visit activities.

Reflection:
Teachers provide feedback on the visit, evaluate findings by using student feedback, and suggest changes when planning the next trip.

So, some freedom of free-choice learning allows students the opportunity to make interdisciplinary inquires and really engage. After the visit, take even a few minutes to debrief students. Talk about what they just learned, do a quick extension activity, or look at the pictures taken during the visit. Allow students to really think about what they learned, and do a quick review about what they just experienced. The following day is the best time to take a more in-depth look at what they had learned, and connect it to what they are learning in class. For post-visit activities, students who had been working in groups could present their findings to the class. These presentations can be supplemented by photographs and videos they took at the ISI. Each student in the group should be asked to participate in the presentation. This helps reinforce what they had learnt at the site, and gives their classmates the opportunity to ask questions and learn together as a community. The worksheets used to collect information at the ISI should be shared by students to complete their project, or used in a written test, which is helpful in satisfying assessment requirements.

Important Points to Remember

Setting the Stage:
- Ensure the trip is linked to the established curriculum.
- Use a variety of methods for introducing a fieldtrip topic to students and clarify the objectives of the trip.
- Create a bulletin board, interest center, or other instructional display to spark interest and encourage students to think about the site.
- Ensure all students take an active role in data gathering during the field trip.

Planning the Fieldtrip:
- Contact ISI staff at the fieldtrip site as early as possible, and share objectives of the visit, and activities to be conducted at the site.
- Appoint chaperones and identify any special needs such as handicapped access.
- Establish rules for fieldtrip behavior prior to the day of the trip, and enforce any rules consistently.

After the Fieldtrip:
- Promote class discussion using photos taken during the trip as prompts.
- Create a hallway display communicating to other classes what was learned during the fieldtrip, or prepare presentations inviting other classes to be your audience.
- Use findings from fieldtrips to prepare a report or portfolio, or set a test under examination conditions.

REFERENCES

Bamberger, Y., & Tal, T. (2007). Learning in a personal-context: Levels of choice in a free-choice learning environment in science and natural history museums. *Science Education, 91*, 75–95.

Campbell, C., & Tytler, R. (2007). Views of student learning. In V. Dawson & G. Venville (Eds.), *The art of teaching primary science* (pp. 23–42). Crows Nest: Allen & Unwin.

Coll, S. D., Coll, R. K., & Treagust, D. F. (2018a). Making the most of out-of-school visits: How does the teacher prepare? Part I: Development of the Learner Integrated Field Trip Inventory (LIFTI). *International Journal of Innovation in Science and Mathematics Education, 26*(4), 1–19.

Coll, S. D., Coll, R. K., & Treagust, D. F. (2018b). Making the most of out-of-school visits: How does the teacher prepare? Part II: Implementation & evaluation of the Learner Integrated Field Trip Inventory (LIFTI). *International Journal of Innovation in Science and Mathematics Education, 26*(4), 20–29.

Dierking, L. D., Falk, J. H., Rennie, L., Anderson, D., & Ellenbogen, K. (2003). Policy statement of the 'Informal Science Education' Ad Hoc Committee. *Journal of Research in Science Teaching, 40*(1), 108–111.

Falk, J. H. (2006). An identity-centred approach to understanding museum learning. *Curator, 49*(2), 151–166.

Falk, J. H., & Dierking, L. (2000). *Learning from museum: Visitors experience and the making of meaning.* Walnut Creek, CA: Alta Mira.

Falk, J. H., & Dierking, L. D. (2012). Lifelong science learning for adults: The role of free-choice experiences. In B. J. Fraser, K. G. Tobin, & C. J. McRobbie (Eds.), *Second international handbook of science education* (Vol. 2, pp. 1063–1079). Dordrecht: Springer.

Farmer, J., Knapp, D., & Benton, G. M. (2007). An elementary school environmental education field trip: Long-term effects on ecological and environmental knowledge and attitude development. *Journal of Environmental Education, 38*(1), 33–42.

CHAPTER 4

Goodrum, D. (2007). Teaching strategies for classroom learning. In V. Dawson & G. Venville (Eds.), *The art of teaching primary science* (pp. 108–126). Crows Nest: Allen & Unwin.

Griffin, J., & Symington, D. (1997). Moving from task-oriented to learning-oriented strategies on school excursions to museums. *Science Education, 81*, 763–779.

Paris, S. (1997). Situated motivation and informal learning. *Journal of Museum Education, 22*(2–3), 22–26.

Rennie, L. J. (2007). Learning science outside of school. In S. K. Abell & N. G. Lederman (Eds.), *Handbook of research in science education* (pp. 125–167). Mahwah, NJ: Lawrence Erlbaum.

Rennie, L. J., & Johnston, D. J. (2007). Research on learning from museum. In J. H. Falk, L. D. Dierking, & S. Foutz (Eds.), *In principle, in practice: Museums as learning institutions* (pp. 57–73). Walnut Creek, CA: Alta Mira Press.

Tal, R. T. (2012). Out-of-school: Learning experiences, teaching and students' learning. In B. J. Fraser, K. G. Tobin, & C. J. McRobbie (Eds.), *Second international handbook of science education* (Vol. 2, pp. 1109–1122). Dordrecht: Springer.

Tal, T., & Morag, O. (2007). School visits to natural history museums: Teaching or enriching. *Journal of Research in Science Teaching, 44*(5), 747–769.

Whittington, A. (2006). Challenging girls' constructions of feminity in the outdoors. *Journal of Experiential Education, 28*(3), 205–221.

CHAPTER 5

INTEGRATING FORMAL, INFORMAL AND NON-FORMAL LEARNING USING THE DIGITALLY-INTEGRATED FIELDTRIP INVENTORY (DIFI)

ABSTRACT

Blended learning offers substantial benefits for both teachers and students, and leads to more rigorous, challenging, engaging, and thought-provoking learning experiences. In this chapter a model of blended learning, the Digitally-Integrated Fieldtrip Inventory (DIFI) is presented. Like the Learner-Integrated Field Trip Inventory (LIFTI) described in Chapter 3, the DIFI comprises Procedural, Social & Cognitive components, all of which must be present in order to maximize the integration of different types of learning.

INTRODUCTION

As seen in Chapter 3, if LEOS are to improve the learning of science, they need to complement not replace in-class/school learning, and need to be part of an integrated curriculum approach to the learning of science. The integration of formal, informal and non-formal learning experiences was described in Chapter 4. In Chapter 5, we show how to integrate in-class and LEOS using another model we developed in our research: the *Digitally-Integrated Fieldtrip Inventory* (DIFI). This integration is achieved by the use of a *Leaning Management System* (LMS). The one we used in our work was *Moodle*, but any LMS can be used. Moodle has some advantages, one being that it is open source. The purpose of using an LMS is that as well as drawing upon LIFTI and combining classroom learning with LEOS, using digital technologies fits well with students' lived experiences and their digital world. We explore this dimension below, when we describe blended learning in more detail.

BLENDED LEARNING

Before delving into the DIFI, let's first look at blended learning more generally, and then draw upon these ideas to see how you can use the DIFI. We are not trying to

CHAPTER 5

cover everything written about blended learning here, but are drawing upon our own experiences and research, and in particular those related to the integration of LEOS and classroom learning.

A blended learning environment is generally viewed as consisting 'blending,' of e-learning (or online learning), and face-to-face learning. In its simplest form, blended learning integrates digital content such as text or video clips, or educational activities such as games, with face-to-face classroom learning. A more formal view sees blended learning as something that integrates digital content with traditional teaching methods. Blended learning typically still requires the physical presence of the teacher and students in a classroom, but gives the student some control over their time, space, and learning path and pace, via e-learning support or teaching. The aim is not to reduce the importance of the teacher, but to provide other ways for teachers to use digital technologies to support learning. The use of digital technologies does not itself result in better learning. Reading text in a hardcopy textbook or in digital form on a tablet or laptop is likely to result in much the same learning outcomes. Didactic teaching, whether face-to-face or captured digitally in videos, is still didactic teaching; again likely to result in much the same learning outcomes. The challenge is to use the power of the digital technologies to *foster better interaction* and *more active learning*, or to use the power of the Internet to source learning materials or activities, fostering self-directed learning, and so on. For this to happen, teachers need to create new learning approaches, and ensure that students readily accept this. This means creating a positive and supportive atmosphere that builds upon students' desire to use digital technologies, which are an integral part of their daily lives, and to embrace the new learning methodologies.

New approaches, successes, and failures with a blended-learning approach emphasize the ever-evolving nature of the teacher's role within the context of the model. A critical need for teachers in this context is that they need to acquire new understandings and skills in using digital technologies themselves if they are to support teaching in a student-centered approach. By giving students a chance to do more than passively sit and absorb information, but instead to create, design and think critically, teachers are not only give them the knowledge to be successful, they are encouraged to create their own path to success. Hopefully, in the process, they learn to better self-assess and reflect, both critical skills needed for success in school teaching, and a teaching career.

We have used a variety of digital technologies in our work, and we will briefly cover these now. Some of these don't need a LMS, so we will look at these first, starting with the use of video clips. In the past blended learning often meant something quite basic, often involving the use of readily available video clips, which were simply projected for students to watch. There is nothing wrong with students watching video clips, but on its own that doesn't achieve much. But if we follow up the viewing of the video clip with some classroom or online activity such as a Forum discussion, students gain from the experience. We can be more creative than that too. When using video clips teachers have two choices. They can use readily available video clips such as those from sites such as YouTube. But teachers also can produce, or allow students to produce, their own video clips. This latter option is not as simple as it might seem, because adjusting to the technical demands of either producing reasonable quality videos, as well as ongoing fine-tuning the model to manage workflow and engage students, requires a major commitment of time, energy, and effort (this plus equipment, although the ubiquitous smartphone can be used). However, the benefit of having students watch or create a video outside of class is that it reserves the class time for discussion and peer collaboration, and moves the teacher to more of a facilitator in the classroom – consistent with constructivist-based teaching. There are tools such as the Forum and the Wiki sites in Moodle, through which students interact with the video and we talk more about that later.

Let's now look more deeply at the use of a LMS such as Moodle. Moodle, is one of a number of systems described as Web 2.0 Technologies,[1] and is used here to refer to a learning platform which allows students to provide evidence-based arguments and explanations, to analyze and synthesize data and to defend their conclusions. Learning Management Systems like Moodle have a variety of valuable learning tools or functionalities. Forum is a discussion site on Moodle, which can be used by teachers and students for group discussion. Wiki is another site on Moodle, where students aided by the teacher co-construct knowledge, following a model like Wikipedia. In both sites teachers can easily track who made what contributions and monitor student interaction.

Of these, we have found the use of Wiki to be most useful; primarily because it helps students engage in interactive learning. It also allows them to critique others ideas, and importantly, to co-construct knowledge, one of the highest level cognitive challenges we can provide. Teachers can create a Wiki for students to build profile pages, share information and respond to discussion threads. The idea is that students can do some of these activities outside of the classroom, and then teachers can plan activities, which provide opportunities to engage students with their classroom peers.

Let's now look at how Wiki and other tools work together to create a more active learning environment. As mentioned earlier, Wiki is one of the collaborative or social network features embedded within Moodle, and activities are easily set up by co-constructing, using Wiki and sharing documents driven by what is called in the literature *New Media Literacies* (NML). The intent of using NML and Web 2.0 Technologies is to support constructivist-based approaches to teaching and learning (Lynman, Billings, Ellinger, Finn, & Perkel, 2005). NML consist of those experiences organized specifically to support formal educational achievement, but they also may be used in informal learning. As we shall see in the use of the DIFI, we can use NML during LEOS, for example, by allowing students to engage in collaboration via Wiki outside classroom hours. This approach formed the basis of much of our own research and approach to the integration of LEOS and classroom learning; viz., our 'version' of blended learning.

There are three features of NML: *Social Presence*, *Social Affordance* and *Transactional Distance*. Let's look at each of these in turn. Learning can be facilitated

CHAPTER 5

in such a way that the perception of *Social Presence* is increased by the use of a LMS. What is meant by that, is teachers create a 'virtual classroom,' where students have a 'digital presence,' in much the same way, they are present in a conventional bricks-and-mortar classroom. This is familiar territory for modern students; it is not unlike their presence in various social media they already engage in their everyday lives (e.g., Facebook). There are some advantages to a digital social presence. Developing a social presence increases the ability to substitute digital-based interactions for face-to-face interactions, while achieving the same or comparable learning outcomes (Gerber, Cavallo, & Marek, 2001; Richardson & Swan, 2003). *Social Affordance*, similarly, is where using a digital platform, students learn more actively; viz., their digital interactions *afford*, or enhance the social component of learning. An example illustrates how this can work better in some cases in a digital environment. Social affordance is often increased in digital environments, because some more shy or reticent students who do not ask questions or speak up in class, are provided with a platform to post their inquiries, which are then answered by their teachers and students in their groups. It is important to note here, that many schools are uneasy about teaching students and in effect encouraging students' to use (or over use) social media, because of concerns such as cyberbullying, cybersecurity, and so on. This feature then assists in reducing what is call *Transactional Distance*, viz., the 'distance' is reduced because they are getting a response from someone who knows more about the question being asked (i.e., a More Knowledgeable Other – MKO),[2] because collaborative learning characterizes informal learning. We found a blended learning environment like this is an effective way of enhancing learning outcomes during LEOS.

In summary, there are different ways teachers can implement blended learning, and this varies depending on the learning environment. It is recommended teachers start with one method or tool. If there are positive effects, for example, more time to collaborate in class and students are more engaged, then continue. If not, the teacher will have still probably come to learn more about the students and their needs and perceptions of learning in a way that might indicate how to best work with them without the use of NML. All teachers need to constantly reflect on teaching methods and encourage self-assessment with students, all being part of learning and growing together. Getting started can take some risk and time. These tools can offer innovative or creative learning methods in the classroom, opening up the time and space for where and when learning occurs. By responding to questions, students become more accountable, and can evidence learning. The teacher gets in-time feedback, and can better understand how the students are learning, and provide more personalized instruction. These tools are great for the teacher to create lessons, but also provide the opportunity for students to create lessons that can be shared with other students. In our experience, these tools have provided a lot of authentic learning, and encourage problem-solving, critical thinking and collaboration. More importantly, they create an opportunity for students to move from learners to become leaders, and from consumers to creators in the classroom. This is one of the main goals as teachers – to provide opportunities that empower students to take more control and drive their own learning. These leadership opportunities also help the students to feel valued because of the work that they are doing.

A final thought about blended learning before moving on to the Digitally Integrated Fieldtrip Inventory (DIFI). Best practices for blending learning classroom is a 'hot topic' of discussion in education circles today, probably because many schools want to see digital technologies used to enhance learning. Much of the discussion focuses on finding clear definitions of what such terms mean, and the benefit for learning. There are many resources on the Internet and other resources teachers can use to educate themselves on this topic – including a diverse selection of books and blogs (see, e.g., https://www.gettingsmart.com/2013/09/120-top-articles-on-blended-learning/). We have as mentioned, only touched on a few we found most useful here. All of these tools are great for finding examples, vignettes, templates, suggested tools and ideas. But, even with all of these options, sometimes it is better for teachers to take a risk and try something on their own. The outcomes will not always be the same for each teacher, classroom or student, but it's at least worth a try! Our experience is that our students quickly know, and genuinely appreciate when we try to be more creative in the classroom, particularly when it involves the use of exciting digital technologies and LEOS.

THE DIGITALLY-INTEGRATED FIELDTRIP INVENTORY (DIFI)

Like the Learner-Integrated Field Trip Inventory (LIFTI), the *Digitally Integrated Fieldtrip Inventory* (DIFI) comprises three components; *Procedural, Social* and *Cognitive*. Figure 5.1 shows the conceptual model of the DIFI.

Remember, the DIFI, incorporates the key elements of the LIFTI; viz., the pre-, during- and post-visit planning along with the integration of formal, non-formal, and informal learning. However, in the case of the LIFTI, integration does not involve the use of digital technologies. In the DIFI, digital technologies are used to *enhance* this integration. What also is needed is to use digital technologies to provide for the *integration of LEOS and classroom learning*. As noted above, digital technologies can be used to allow learning activities to be done asynchronously, with the digital-supported activities conducted out of normal classroom hours, allowing more time in class to foster active learning. Each component of the DIFI is now described in turn.

Procedural

The implementation of the *Procedural* component of the DIFI, essentially follows the same approach used in the LIFTI; however, digital technologies are used to foster integration, by setting up Forum pages for each student group. Students are tasked with answering two questions posted on Forum. After getting them to interact with each other, teachers moderate their postings. Advance organizers obtained from the ISI are posted on Forum for student information. Student groups are then

CHAPTER 5

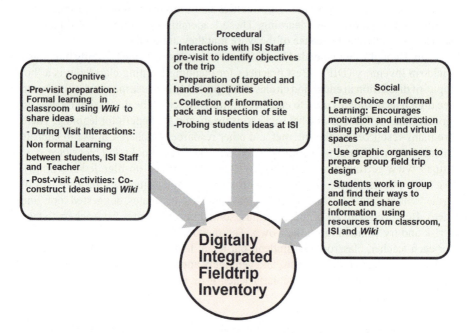

Figure 5.1. The Digitally-Integrated Fieldtrip Inventory (DIFI)

created on Wiki, and students asked to identify the different roles they would take on, pre- during- and post-visit. They also are asked to develop questions further for inquiry at the ISI. These questions from students and those prepared by teachers are used to prepare worksheets, which are posted on Wiki. Students are asked to collect information at the ISI using the worksheets (examples of these are provided in Part 2). Information collected pre- and during-visit is presented post-visit. The information is used by all students to prepare for the written end-of-unit test after the ISI visit.

Social

In our implementation of the *Social* component of the DIFI, student online groups were formed in Moodle using Forum, and the fun experiences they enjoyed at the ISI were reflected in their Moodle postings, which acted as a stimulus for more in depth learning (Rennie, 2007). Students groupings were engineered to encourage active interaction and experience, and substantive discussions (as noted earlier, we used mixed-ability groups, but with some student choice). The students in their groups constructed a plan using the advanced organizer of how they wanted to work, with whom, and the inquiries they wished to make, which were shared using Wiki. Looking at their interactions on Moodle, we could see the students enjoyed learning and engaging in socially-mediated learning environments, where they have both choice and control of what they are doing. This is similar to what Bamberger and Tal (2007, p. 75) reported "students connected the visit to their own life experiences and to their prior knowledge, even when the guided activity scarcely addressed it." When our students visited the ISI to collect information to complete their projects, they were provided with a directory of what they could see and/or do. The students were allowed to choose what they wanted to study, and to explore their individual interests, as noted in the *Cognitive* component of the DIFI (see next section).

Cognitive

In our implementation of the *Cognitive* component of the DIFI, we again used digital technologies to enhance the LIFTI approach. So, for the pre-visit activities, in-class activities were completed prior to the visit, and were directly related to the learning goals for the visit. These comprised online activities using Moodle, and discussions employed a blended learning approach. In particular, we used the Wiki feature of Moodle described above to foster co-construction of knowledge. Pre-visit activities related to during-visit and the post-visit tasks, and, for example, provided students with exposure to a range of scientific theories as suggested by Preston and Rooy (2007). Examples are given in Part 2. Likewise, for during-visit activities, these activities were directly related to the Pre-visit Activities, and again were conducted using Wiki. Consistent with the LIFTI, some freedom of choice was allowed, to ensure better learning outcomes (Falk & Dierking, 2000). For example, students had the opportunity of exploring topics of their own interest, which were not assessed, consistent with the notion of free-choice learning. Finally, for the post-visit activities, classroom activities were developed to consolidate learning, which occurred during LEOS. Each group was asked to complete their worksheet on Wiki, which was then presented to the class as a post-visit report. This report was accompanied by photographs and videos of ISI staff presentations.

The post-visit activities provided students with understanding of how the LEOS related to their classroom learning, and subsequently used the findings to complete a project-based assessment task. These discussions continued in a blended learning environment.

Multifaceted Roles of the Teacher in the Implementation of the Digitally Integrated Fieldtrip Inventory (DIFI)

To show you how this all works, let's look at the role the teacher played in the implementation of the DIFI. This is presented as a narrative, which details the experiences of some teachers who worked with us in the implementation of the LIFTI and DIFI.

CHAPTER 5

Some Year 11 classroom teachers were asked to create a Forum site on the LMS, where students first shared their thoughts on topical and personal issues on a daily basis. This was intended to provide an opportunity for induction to this new pedagogical tool, especially for social networking (at this stage the students had not used Moodle previously). The teachers were encouraged to make an effort to add to Forum themselves on a regular (at least daily) basis, so that students could see and value the 'presence' of their teacher in their social networks. The teachers were asked to write comments in such a way as to make students feel valued, heard, and to create a culture where students willingly shared their daily events. Students who failed to contribute, were approached informally in person to identify what the teacher could do to get them involved. The Wiki pages were then used to introduce students to the topic of interest, such as Ecology. This provided an opportunity to identify student's prior knowledge in this subject area, a key aspect of constructivist-based teaching. The classroom lessons were still used for formal learning, where students used textbooks and teacher guidance to develop a deeper understanding of this topic.

The sort of social networking questions posted on Forum were:

- Where did you go on the school fieldtrip? What were some features of the trip you did not like? What suggestions can help improve these types of trips?
- How many students have visited an ecological reserve? What is special about this site? Would it be a place you would consider visiting one day, why or why not?
- Share any Māori[3] myths and legends that surround this ecological reserve, and
- If you had the opportunity to create a sanctuary, what are some of the features you would be considering when building it?

Likewise, the teachers promoted learning, and the co-construction of knowledge, by starting the Wiki. Some group learning questions on the Wiki site pre-visit were:

- What is a socio-scientific issue?
- How do I form a research question for my issue?

To drive effective use of LEOS based on the DIFI, there were a number of new media literacies we used (viz., video clips, Forum & Wiki), and our pedagogies were linked to our understanding of effective learning covered in the earlier chapters. This does change things from the conventional classroom, and we now finish off this Chapter by looking at this.

First, you need to redefine your role in the classroom. In a blended learning environment you use conventional tools and digital tools alongside each other, and remember the learning can, and should be, asynchronous to free up class time. Choose appropriate components of your LMS; as mentioned we used video clips, Forum and Wiki. The digital content should complement learning objectives, and help achieve the intended learning outcomes. If it doesn't, the tool is irrelevant and likely ineffectual. The tool, though, also needs to be fun. Students won't use a tool they don't like. In our case we inducted students using Forum, a type of activity they were already familiar with (i.e., like blogging). Create individual and collective learning goals. You need to establish an overarching learning goal, but supplement this with individual learning goals. Students work at different paces, and each student will have their own learning path. Learn to incorporate that information into your blended learning planning to drive success with individual students and the whole class. Develop a classroom culture that embraces blended learning. We use the acronym TRICK, which stands for *T*rust, *R*espect, *I*ndependence, *C*ollaboration, and *K*indness. With these values embedded in the classroom, students want to learn, grow, and help out their teacher and classmates. Set expectations, students achieve when given goals, so set expectations. Let them know how to succeed in the classroom and at home, and they will. Finally, provide clear instructions and routines.

Consistent with the constructivist notion of the teacher as both teacher and facilitator, you need to give students control over time, path, place, and pace of learning. It can be hard to relinquish control, but students succeed when given the chance to direct their learning. They become more engaged with the content, because they have a personal stake in their own success. As suggested throughout this chapter and the previous chapter, encourage collaboration in the classroom and online. Collaboration gives students the chance to work through complex concepts, and to help each other learn. It also offers opportunities for dialogue, which teaches students to position their points with facts and hard evidence. Collaboration should occur in the classroom and online; quieter students, for example, often become extremely 'vocal' when online.

Use the power of LEOS to incite curiosity, imagination, and critical thinking. Students start wondering and thinking when you ask, 'What if?' You can raise that question through traditional teaching methods and online content. The more you ask open-ended and thought-provoking questions, the more students are driven to seek out answers. You can then leverage the LMS functionality to challenge students to learn and grow with authentic, relevant tasks. Give students real, curriculum-based, challenging assignments, and they will complete, and compete, to finish them.

As the driver of knowledge construction, you need to review classroom and online content regularly. Online content supplements other teaching methods, it doesn't replace them. This is particularly important if you allow students to use the Internet to source resources. As such, you should go over both content and student postings to evaluate students' basic comprehension and deepen understanding. You need to measure individual and classroom progress. Blended learning leads to real impact when it's measured. The work should be fairly easy to do, because as noted above at this stage, you already decided on goals, objectives, and outcomes. Analyze classroom impact to balance traditional teaching time and student (i.e., finding a sensible point on a continuum from fully face-to-face to fully online). Every classroom is different, so take some time to find the right balance of traditional teaching methods and the use of digital media. Many teachers start with a 50/50 blend and work from there. As mentioned above, it is worthwhile taking some risks in your approach, and you

CHAPTER 5

don't have to do exactly what we did! Identify new goals and objectives, and repeat. Once you measure progress and impact, you may discover that learning goals need to change. That's a good thing. Goals can and should change over time. However, any change means you'll need to continually adjust teaching methods and digital content to see continued success with blended learning. Not surprisingly, you need to communicate with everyone. A blended learning classroom requires communication with everyone—students, professionals, peers, administrators, and parents. Blending learning works best when everybody shares a belief in the vision for it. Don't forget your helpers, especially the students' parents/guardians and older caregivers: Help them out with an evening class or individual meetings. By interacting with them on a personal level, you'll see interest, buy-in, and participation grow at home and in the classroom.

Finally, be patient, remember that it takes time to succeed with blended learning.

Important Points to Remember

- The integration of LEOS and classroom learning can and should be facilitated by the use of digital technologies.
- Most LMS have a variety of tools or functionality such as Forum and Wiki, which can be used to increase social presence, provide affordances for learning, and reduces transactional distance.
- Use of the DIFI requires redefining the role of the teacher, to be consistent with a constructivist approach, as a facilitator of learning.

As discussed in Chapter 5, we created a conceptual model called Digitally Field Trip Inventory (DIFI) to maximize learning opportunities from Learning Experiences outside the Classroom (LEOS). In summary, the DIFI model is made up of three components; namely Procedural, Cognitive and Social.

The Procedural component is further made up of four sub-components:

- Interaction with ISI staff pre-visit to identify objectives of the trip.
- Preparations of hands-on and targeted activities.
- Collection of information pack and inspection of the ISI site.
- Probing students' ideas when at the ISI.

The Cognitive component is made up of three sub-components:

- Pre-visit: Preparation includes formal learning in the classroom using Wiki.
- During-Visit: Non-formal learning at the ISI.
- Post-visit: Co-constructing ideas using Wiki.

The Social component is made up of three sub-components:

- Allow free choice/informal learning to encourage motivation and interactions using both physical and virtual spaces.

- Use resources from the ISI as organizers to prepare group fieldtrip design.
- Students work in groups, collaborate and share resources collected from the classroom, ISI site and from Wiki.

Whilst there are three key components in this model, discussions with teachers suggested that it would be easier to prepare and use lesson plans using three key terms, namely pre-, during and post-visit planning. This practice is aligned with the way preparations for fieldtrips are conducted around the world. These three key terms will encompass the three key components and sub-components of the DIFI model, which are now presented in Part 2.

NOTES

[1] Web 2.0 Technologies is a term used for second generation web-based systems, and are characterized by active functionality, such as social media (Facebook & others are familiar Web 2.0 Technologies).
[2] See https://www.simplypsychology.org/vygotsky.html
[3] Māori are people that self-identify as Indigenous New Zealanders.

REFERENCES

Bamberger, Y., & Tal, T. (2007). Learning in a personal-context: Levels of choice in a free-choice learning environment in science and natural history museums. *Science Education, 91*, 75–95.

Falk, J., & Dierking, L. (2000). *Learning from museum: Visitors experience and the making of meaning.* Walnut Creek, CA: Alta Mira.

Gerber, B. L., Cavallo, A. M. L., & Marek, E. A. (2001). Relationships amoung informal learning environments, teaching procedures and scientific reasoning ability. *International Journal of Science Education, 23*(5), 535–549.

Lyman, P., Billings, A., Ellinger, S., Finn, M., & Perkel, D. (2005). *Literature review of kids' informal learning and digital-mediated experiences.* White paper for the MacArthur Foundation. Retrieved from https://www.exploratorium.edu/research/digitalkids/Lyman_DigitalKids.pdf

Preston, C., & Rooy, V. (2007). Planning to teach primary science. In V. Dawson & G. Venville (Eds.), *The art of teaching primary science* (pp. 87–107). Crows Nest: Allen & Unwin.

Rennie, L. J. (2007). Learning science outside of school. In S. K. Abell & N. G. Lederman (Eds.), *Handbook of research in science education* (pp. 125–167). Mahwah, NJ: Lawrence Erlbaum.

Richardson, J. C., & Swan, K. (2003). Examining social presence in online courses in relation to students perceived learning and satisfaction. *Journal of Asynchronous Learning Networks, 7*(1), 68–87.

PART 2

THE PRACTICE OF LEARNING EXPERIENCES OUTSIDE SCHOOL

PART 2

CHAPTER 6

LEARNING BIOLOGICAL SCIENCES VIA LEARNING EXPERIENCES OUTSIDE SCHOOL

ABSTRACT

In this chapter lesson plans are provided for a topic related to local ecosystems, covering the Concept, Task, and Pedagogy to be used. The topic was 'Investigate the biological impact of an event on a New Zealand ecosystem', and the LEOS trip was to an ecological reserve. The lesson plans include details of pre-, during- and post-visit activities for teachers, students and ISI staff.

INTRODUCTION

Part 1 provided the background for the two models used in the implementation of LEOS. In this Section, beginning with this Chapter, are now provided exemplars on the implementation of the DIFI model, for the main subject areas in secondary school science. These subject areas are labelled: *Biological Sciences*, *Chemical Sciences*, *Earth & Space Sciences*, and *Physical Sciences*. These terms are deliberately broad, and do not actually represent the 'learning areas' in the curriculum used in our own context (i.e., New Zealand). For example, in New Zealand, what is called Earth & Space Sciences above, is referred to as *Planet Earth & Beyond* in the secondary school curriculum. The reason these board terms are used in each of the chapters of Part 2, is so teachers can relate the topics to their own learning areas (and labels) in the curriculum documents used in their context. In the exemplars we will refer to the learning areas of the New Zealand Curriculum. Teachers should draw upon the learning areas from their own curriculum when looking at what we have done, and see how they can modify and adapt ours to suit their own context, so the lesson plans and other documentation will be a little different. We have tried to use topics of wide international interest and importance like endangered species and nanotechnology to make this as broadly applicable as possible.

These exemplars follow the DIFI, and as noted in the end of Chapter 5, this is presented as pre- during- and post-visit activities, all integrated using the DIFI. First is provided the Achievement Standard from the New Zealand Curriculum for each topic. This is intended to show how the topic and activities used during the LEOS fits into the bigger picture of the learning area from the curriculum. Then is provided a lesson plan for each topic (using the learning area label from the New Zealand Curriculum), and this is followed by some background about the learning area, so teachers can see the link between the curriculum and the broader topic. Next

© KONINKLIJKE BRILL NV, LEIDEN, 2019 | DOI:10.1163/9789004411760_006 is presented each component of the LEOS; pre-visit, during-visit, and post visit in tabular form, and each phase of the LEOS is linked by the DIFI components viz., *Procedural*, *Social*, and *Cognitive*. We have provided a few photos or illustrations from our LEOS trips to the ISI to give teachers a better understanding of the nature of the particular ISIs we visited, and the pre- and post-visit activities we used.

BIOLOGICAL SCIENCES

Biological sciences cover numerous topics, many of which are multidisciplinary in nature. Many topics also relate well to everyday life; flora and fauna are part of student's lives, and so are of intrinsic interest. The Achievement Standard we used in our LEOS for Biological Sciences relates to something of current worldwide interest – threats to local ecosystems (Table 6.1).[1] Students are easily motivated by such topics, and frequently become emotionally connected to threats to the environment; particularly to living things, and especially to mammals.

Table 6.1. Sample achievement standard – Biological Sciences

Number	AS90951		Version	1
	Achievement Standard			
Subject Reference	Science 1.12			
Title	Investigate the biological impact of an event on a New Zealand ecosystem			
Level 1	Credits 4		Assessment	Internal
Subfield	Science			
Domain	Science – Core			
This achievement standard involves investigating the biological impact of an event on a New Zealand ecosystem.				

Achievement Criteria

Achievement	Achievement with Merit	Achievement with Excellence
Investigate the biological impact of an event on New Zealand ecosystem	Investigate, in depth, the biological impact of an event on a New Zealand ecosystem	Investigate comprehensively, the biological impact of an event on a New Zealand ecosystem

The Achievement Standard also contains 'explanatory notes' and links to the broader curriculum. It defines an event in this context saying, "an event may include natural events such as floods, drought, seasonal changes, landslides and fire; or human actions such as pest control, application of fertilizers, trampling, urbanization, or pollution." The nature of the achievement criteria also are defined. To *investigate*, "involves describing observations or findings, using those findings to identify changed environmental factors, and describing how the changed environmental factors might affect organisms within the ecosystem." To *investigate in depth*, "involves using findings and biological ideas to make causal links between changed environmental factors, and the ecological characteristic or process to explain the impact on organisms or implications for the ecosystem as a whole." To *investigate comprehensively*, "involves using findings and biological ideas to make significant causal links between changed environmental factors and the ecological characteristic or process to discuss the:

- Impact on the organisms
- Implications for the ecosystem as a whole.

It may involve explaining, elaborating, applying, justifying, relating, evaluating, comparing and contrasting, and analyzing." Finally, it is noted that "environmental factors about which information is collected may include: moisture levels, light intensity, temperature, stream clarity, food availability, competition, predation, wave and wind action, shelter, and oxygen levels," and "ecological characteristics and processes may include: food chains/webs, variety of organisms (diversity), nutrient cycles, water cycle, energy flow, interrelationships (predation, parasitism, mutualism), density, distribution pattern, and key species."

Based on this Achievement Standard, we developed a Lesson Plan (Table 6.2), and subsequently implemented this plan using the DIFI, for each of pre-, during- and post-visit activities (Tables 6.3–6.5). In Figures 6.1 and 6.2, we see students interacting with the ISI staff (following the activities and pre-visit briefing given by

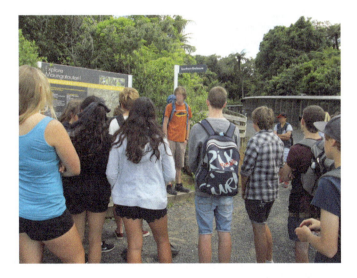

Figure 6.1. Students listening to ISI staff presentation during an LEOS at an ecological reserve

CHAPTER 6

Figure 6.2. Students observing a 1000+ year old tree during an LEOS at an ecological reserve

Table 6.2. Lesson plan for achievement standard in Biological Sciences

---

This Achievement Standard involves investigating the biological impact of an event on a New Zealand ecosystem.

Concept	Environmental sustainability is ensuring that in meeting our need for water, food, shelter as well as engaging in activities that make our lives enjoyable, including leisure activities and entertainment – we do not cause damage to our environment or deplete resources that we cannot renew. There are natural events such as floods, drought, seasonal changes, landslides and fire; or human actions such as pest control, application of fertilizers, trampling, urbanization, or pollution, which affect organisms within the ecosystem.
	It is important that students are made aware of the ecological characteristics and processes which may include: food chains/webs, variety of organisms (diversity), nutrient cycles, water cycle, and energy flow, interrelationships (predation, parasitism, and mutualism), density, distribution pattern, and key species in the ecosystem.
	Some of the environmental factors which need to be learnt are: moisture levels, light intensity, temperature, stream clarity, food availability, competition, predation, wave and wind action, shelter, and oxygen levels, and how these affect organisms and their existence in the defined ecosystem.

(cont.)

Table 6.2. Lesson plan for achievement atandard in Biological Sciences (cont.)

Task	Use findings and biological ideas to produce a report which makes significant *causal* links between changed environmental factors and the ecological characteristic or process. In your report discuss the: • Impact on the organisms • Implications for the ecosystem as a whole. This necessitates explaining, elaborating, applying, justifying, relating, evaluating, comparing and contrasting, and analyzing information collected.
Pedagogy	Create a Wiki page on Moodle, and establish groups. Questions posted on Wiki are: • Why should we have an ecological reserve? • How is an ecological reserve different from a natural forest? Encourage reflective thought and action by taking learning outside school and communicating between teachers and students using Moodle. Taking action is a key component of *Education for Sustainability*[2] and support the development of all the key competencies as students develop their *Action Competence*.[3] Environment consists of our surroundings, made up of air, water, and land, plants and animals, people, their communities, and their social and cultural values. Education about and for the environment must strongly promote the need for personal initiatives, and social participation to achieve sustainability. The curriculum should encourage teachers to adopt a multidisciplinary approach to learning that develops the knowledge, awareness, attitudes, values, and skills that will enable individuals and the community to contribute towards maintaining and improving the quality of the environment. Student should develop: • Awareness and sensitivity to the environment and related issues • Knowledge and understanding of the environment and the impact of people on it • Attitudes and values that reflect feelings of concern for the environment • Skills involved in identifying, investigating, and problem solving associated with environmental issues • A sense of responsibility through participation and action as individuals, or members of groups, *whānau*,[4] or *iwi*,[5] in addressing environmental issues.

CHAPTER 6

Table 6.3. Pre-visit activities for achievement standard in Biological Sciences

Students	Used school and council library, and parents/grandparents to find information on two questions (see 'Task' in Table 6.2). Used this information for classroom discussion, and provided feedback on Moodle Wiki site. Explored YouTube and other New Zealand websites such as Ministry of Primary Industries, New Zealand Forest & Bird, Environment Waikato, Maungatautari Ecological Island Reserve[6] to gain extra information. Asked parents/guardians to join LEOS as chaperones. Prepared a list of questions as a group, which were explored at the ISI. Some of these questions were used by the teacher to prepare a class worksheet. Students were allowed freedom of choice to prepare questions, some which were not formally assessed. These questions were used to prepare the class worksheet. *Class Worksheet* • What is an Island Ecological Reserve? • How big is Island Ecological Reserve? • Name four pest species that were common in Island Ecological Reserve but have been eradicated. How did they know those pests were present and how did they get rid of them? • Name three native plant and three native animal species that are currently on Island Ecological Reserve • Explain the likely outcomes if pests, such as rats, were to get into the enclosure • Discuss the history and development of the Island Ecological Reserve • Name three events which affects the native species of both plants and animals • Are there any disadvantages to the other species if pests are eradicated? • How are organisms interdependent on one another and their environment? • What is biodiversity, and why is it important to conserve it? • How many people are employed and how much are they paid? [not assessed] • What qualification is needed to find employment at an ecological reserve? [not assessed].
Teachers	Assisted students to learn basic ecological principles and develop attitudes, and positive actions towards the fragile nature of New Zealand's biodiversity. Divided students into groups they wished to work with, to discuss and prepare questions for the class worksheet. Posted class worksheet on Wiki, to extend discussions outside classroom hours, and moderated posts to provide support and probe for deeper understanding. Took students on trip to Maungatautari, used to study biodiversity, pest control and breeding programs. Allowed students to walk around a fenced mountain where all pests had been eradicated. A variety of flora and fauna including, exotic reptiles, such as the *Tuatara* were seen when exploring the sanctuary. Teachers encouraged students to record information using a recorder/smartphone, and to take photographs to be used in their reports.

(cont.)

Table 6.3. Pre-visit activities for achievement standard in Biological Sciences (cont.)

	Contacted ISI staff to arrange the fieldtrip. Upon confirmation, teachers informed students about this, and started developing objectives for the visit by linking them to work completed in class.
	Prepared consent forms, informed school office and completed all required outdoor documents, student medication and first aid kit, arranged transportation, meals and invited parents/guardians to be chaperones.
	Grouped students, and provided a list of names to the ISI staff for each group, to allow them to identify individuals and communicate with different students post-visit if students needed more information or support. This list was also given to the chaperones.
	Provided a class worksheet to the ISI staff before the school visit.
ISI Staff	With teachers who visited the site, identified safety related issues, and provided ISI information pack (downloaded from the website: https://www.sanctuarymountain.co.nz/educate-us).
	Agreed on Shared Objectives of the visit. ISI staff were asked to prepare and discuss how: • Natural events such as floods, drought, seasonal changes, landslides and fire; or human actions such as pest control, application of fertilizers, trampling, urbanization, or pollution affects species biodiversity • Environmental factors such as moisture levels, light intensity, temperature, stream clarity, food availability, competition, predation, wave and wind action, shelter, and oxygen levels affect species biodiversity • Ecological characteristics and processes: food chains/webs, variety of organisms (diversity), nutrient cycles, water cycle, energy flow, interrelationships (predation, parasitism, mutualism), density, distribution pattern, affect species biodiversity.

the ISI staff – see Table 6.3), and during the visit experiencing the dramatic sight of a 1000+ year old majestic tree.

REFLECTIONS AND CONCLUSIONS

As we have seen, this Achievement Standard involves investigating the biological impact of an event on a New Zealand ecosystem. Following the DIFI, we now provide some refection we made after evaluation of the whole LEOS for this topic, and seek to draw some conclusions. This is a key feature of good teaching, and should always be employed when doing something different or innovative. In other work we have done, we used a guide called the FAR Guide (*F*ocus, *A*ction & *R*eflection) (Harrison & Coll, 2008, pp. 127–174) to help teach science better using analogies. A key feature of the

CHAPTER 6

Table 6.4. During-visit activities for achievement standard in Biological Sciences

Students	Worked in groups to find answers to complete the class worksheet (Table 6.3).
	Were encouraged, by teachers to approach ISI staff to seek further support, and use other websites to help extend their knowledge.
	Recorded information using a recorder/smartphone and took photographs, which were used in their studies/reports. Students uploaded these images and websites on Wiki for both teacher and feedback from other members in their group.
Teachers	Facilitated group discussions by probing student ideas, and encouraged deeper thinking: • Why do we need to preserve biodiversity? • What would happen if we did not manage destruction of rainforests to build residential areas? • What role does government play in ensuring our country maintains a rich biodiversity? • Are there any universities who are currently working with this ISI to preserve biodiversity? • If so, how are they doing this?
ISI Staff	Engaged students using multimedia resources, and probed students' response.
	Prepared presentations on three Shared Objectives (Table 6.3).
	Used the topic: '*Should 1080 be used to kill possums in the New Zealand bush?*' The presentation included MAFF websites, videos and realia (i.e., objects or activities used to relate classroom teaching to real life) – in this case stuffed possums, baits, cages, testimonies from farmers, possum lovers, and so on.
	Used student list to identify students, and allowed quiet students to help assist in the presentation and to facilitate group discussions, distribute items, hold charts, and use pointers to show places or objects discussed on the Power-Point.
	Encouraged students to ask questions.

FAR Guide is reflection on what worked and what did not work after the teaching event. This helps us continuously refine the pedagogy and logistics of LEOS.

The teacher obtained feedback on the visit, evaluating findings by using student feedback from classroom discussions and postings on Wiki. Examples of student feedback included:

- Need more information on 1080 poisoning, and how it affected both plant and animal species
- Need to know how each of the event namely floods, drought, seasonal changes, landslides and fire; or human actions such as pest control, application of fertilizers, trampling, urbanization, or pollution affected both a native plant and animal species

Table 6.5. Post-visit activities for achievement standard in Biological Sciences

Students	Provided evidence-based arguments and explanations, to each other's postings on Wiki.
	Presented their work in class, and were quizzed by students from other groups.
	After these presentations, and with more classroom lessons with teachers, completed their portfolio.
	Some instead completed an assessment for two hours under examination conditions, drawing upon information from group pages on Wiki, to complete an end-of-unit test.
Teachers	Re-visited the objectives of the fieldtrip, and identified in discussion with students, types of information collected from the ISI.
	Linked student feedback to the objectives of the visit, and the assessment task.
	Moderated student work on Moodle, to ensure they achieved the intended learning objectives for the unit.
	Placed emphasis on how natural disasters (those selected) impact on organisms, and the implications of ecosystems as a whole.
	Marked a minimum of five student reports, and these were subsequently moderated by peer-teachers or the Head of Department. If teacher marking agreed with that of moderator, the teacher continued to use the marking schedule, and completed marking all student reports.

- Lessons in the classroom mainly focused on animals while those at the ISI did not include all environmental factors and ecological characteristics and processes.

The teacher also considered ways of better facilitating discussions with ISI staff, so all Shared Objectives of the visit could be adequately addressed. Here feedback included:

- ISI staff should focus on *all* biological ideas and make causal links between changed environmental factors (which may include moisture levels, light intensity, temperature, stream clarity, food availability, competition, predation, wave and wind action, shelter, and oxygen levels), and the ecological characteristic (may include food chains/webs, variety of organisms (diversity), nutrient cycles, water cycle, energy flow, interrelationships (predation, parasitism, mutualism), density, distribution pattern), and key species.

The discussion at the ISI also should involve the impact on the organisms, and the implications for the ecosystem as a whole. An example is the release of 1080 poison (i.e., an 'event'), would seek to eradicate possums, and increase the chances of survival of native tress, which in turn affects food availability to birds, hence population density and competition for food, between species. Also, probing

CHAPTER 6

students' ideas during group discussions so that they could get more information from the ISI staff. Accessing information from the website as well as the ISI staff which would assist in better preparing students for the visit.

Finally, the teacher felt that to develop citizens who take care of living and non-living resources, it is essential students see themselves as part of the environment. Students need to be able to see the interdependence of living and non-living things, understand the importance of sustainability, and its impact on biodiversity, and begin realizing personal and social responsibility for action. So in-class work needs to involve students researching on all changed environmental factors, and the ecological characteristic or processes to explain the impact on organisms or implications for the ecosystem as a whole, and not just the ones they selected to study and report on. This also included having them as part of the environment and explaining to the class, as well as posting on Wiki, influences these changes had on them as an individual which included impacts on agricultural food source, bush walks, places to swim and camping sites, fishing in lakes and oceans, and ambient temperature.

NOTES

[1] See https://www.nzqa.govt.nz/ncea/subjects/science/annotated-exemplars/level-1-as90951/
[2] See http://sustainableschoolsproject.org/education
[3] See http://www.tlri.org.nz/sites/default/files/projects/9245_Appendix%20E.pdf
[4] A Māori term general taken to mean extended family, but actually more complex, see https://teara.govt.nz/en/whanau-maori-and-family/page-1
[5] A Māori term generally taken to mean a tribe, but more accurately a set of people bound together by descent from a common ancestor or ancestors, see https://teara.govt.nz/en/glossary#1
[6] See https://www.sanctuarymountain.co.nz/sitemap; https://www.forestandbird.org.nz/; https://www.waikatoregion.govt.nz/

REFERENCE

A. G. Harrison & R. K. Coll (Eds.), (2008). *Using analogies in middle and secondary science classrooms.* Thousand Oaks, CA: Corwin.

CHAPTER 7

LEARNING CHEMICAL SCIENCES VIA LEARNING EXPERIENCES OUTSIDE SCHOOL

ABSTRACT

In this chapter lesson plans are provided for a topic related to air pollution, covering the Concept, Task, and Pedagogy to be used. The topic was 'Demonstrate understanding of the chemistry in a technological application', and the LEOS trip was to a nanotechnology research institute. The lesson plans include details of pre-, during- and post-visit activities for teachers, students and ISI staff.

INTRODUCTION

The second learning area is Chemical Sciences. Like Biological Sciences, this is quite broad in scope, and there are a wide variety of topics taught under such a broad heading. Similarly, there are many topics, which are multidisciplinary in nature, such as pollution, materials chemistry, catalysts, and nanotechnology; such topics often lend themselves well to LEOS. Multidisciplinary topics also often are easier to relate to everyday life (like catalytic converters in motor vehicles), and because of this they are of greater interest to students. The Achievement Standard used here relates using chemistry in a technological application (Table 7.1).

CHEMICAL SCIENCES

Students often see this area as 'pure chemistry' and fail to understand how diverse the subject/discipline is, and how chemistry and related subjects impact upon all of the other sciences and upon everyday life (Dalgety & Coll, 2004). We often hear people talking about natural and synthetic substances as if they are different, and the term 'organic' is often used in terms of foods in a sense that it is better than something 'manufactured' or 'artificial.' It is critical that chemistry teaching dispels common unscientific beliefs that chemicals are somehow bad or dangerous. One of the best ways to do this, as with any science teaching, is to show how chemistry relates to everyday life. Literally everything, including ourselves is made up of chemicals. From a scientific perspective, there is no difference between a natural or synthetic chemicals. Modern chemistry teaching thus seeks to link chemistry and chemicals to everyday life, and one good way to do this is to look at the application of chemistry to technology or to solve technical or social problems. This helps students understand that chemistry and chemicals are

CHAPTER 7

not inherently evil, and that what matters is understanding the chemicals, and their chemistry, and using them for our benefit and the benefit of others.

The Achievement Standard used here was deliberately chosen to show how the application of chemistry could help address an important societal issue. In this case, that of air pollution. Like the example we used for the Biological Sciences in Chapter 6, air pollution is something all students will be familiar with, and quite likely concerned about. The use of an ISI during the LEOS allows us to link this to a modern and exciting area of interest in Chemical Sciences, that of nanotechnology. This gets regular attention in the media, so it is likely to be very appealing to students.

Table 7.1. Sample achievement standard – Chemical Sciences

Number	AS90931	Version	3
	Achievement Standard		
Subject Reference	Chemistry 1.2		
Title	Demonstrate understanding of the chemistry in a technological application		
Level 1	Credits 2	Assessment	Internal
Subfield	Science		
Domain	Chemistry		

This achievement standard involves demonstrating understanding of the chemistry in a technological application.

Achievement Criteria

Achievement	Achievement with Merit	Achievement with Excellence
Demonstrate understanding of the chemistry in a technological application	Demonstrate in-depth understanding of the chemistry in a technological application	Demonstrate comprehensive understanding of the chemistry in a technological application

As with the exemplar for Biological Sciences (Table 6.1), there are explanatory notes provided for the Chemistry Achievement Standard AS90931.[1] A *technological application*, "means a use of chemistry to meet the needs of society. Examples include – food and beverage chemistry, acids and bases in the home and/or in industry, sources of energy, cosmetics, detergents, pharmaceuticals. The chosen technological application must be based on situations that involve chemical principles." Likewise, *demonstrating understanding*, "typically involves providing characteristics of, or an account of, the chemistry related to the use of the chosen application." *Demonstrating in-depth understanding*, "typically involves explaining how or why the chemistry applies to the use of the chosen application." *Demonstrating comprehensive understanding*, "typically involves linking the chemistry applicable to the chosen application with its use. The linking may include explaining, elaborating, justifying, relating, evaluating, comparing and contrasting, or analyzing."

Based on this Achievement Standard, we developed a lesson plan (Table 7.2), and subsequently implemented this plan using the DIFI, for each of pre-, during- and post-visit activities (Tables 7.3–7.5). Again we provide some illustrations, where we see how students interacted with the ISI staff (following the activities and pre-visit briefing given by the ISI staff – see Table 7.2), and during the visit.

The students were asked to demonstrate their understanding of the chemistry involved in a technological application, using a format of their choice, such as a poster, Power-Point presentation, Wiki, or Blog. Further contexts such as manufacture of superphosphate or visiting a nanotechnology laboratory could also be considered; this latter resource was chosen for the reasons now provided.

Challenges facing New Zealand (and many other countries) are access to clean water, production of renewable energy, and dealing with the potential effects of climate change. Although societal choices are undoubtedly part of the problem and solution (e.g., changes in behavior), addressing these issues means we need new materials, and new technology that may be based on materials that have not yet been discovered. The New Zealand *MacDiarmid Institute for Advanced Materials and Nanotechnology* is an institution which schools can visit to learn about the development, and use of how new materials can improve people's lives, and this was the ISI used for this topic (Figures 7.1 & 7.2).

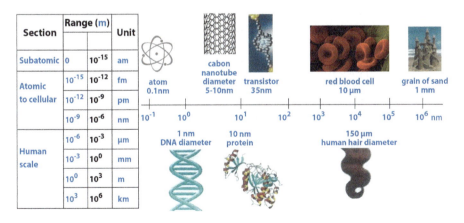

Figure 7.1. Details from slide on nanotechnology shown to students visiting the MacDiarmid Institute for Advanced Materials and Nanotechnology (produced by Sereima Raimua, graphic designer, University of South Pacific)

CHAPTER 7

Group activity: Feynman's challenge

In a famous speech 'There is plenty of room at the bottom', Richard Feynman raised the possibility to print the entire content of Encyclopedia Britannica on a pin's head. Reason whether this could, in principle, be done. Discuss the issues in your team and prepare to report back in ~20 min.
Useful data:
- EB has ~30 volumes, each ~1,000 pages
- page size 27.9 cm × 21.6 cm
- diameter of a pin's head: 1.5 mm
- smallest feature in print: full stop '.' (has diameter 0.2 mm)

Figure 7.2. Task put to students visiting the MacDiarmid Institute for Advanced Materials and Nanotechnology

Table 7.2. Lesson plan for achievement standard in Chemical Sciences

This Achievement Standard involves demonstrating understanding of the chemistry of a technological application in New Zealand.

Concept	Chemistry is an important part of the world around us. Nanotechnology, is a branch of chemistry that looks at chemistry of small systems. One nanometer, is a billionth or 10^{-9} of a meter. Scientists have found that atoms and molecules behave quite differently at the nanoscale. Nanotechnology is a rapidly expanding field, and scientists and engineers are currently making materials at the nanoscale to take advantage of enhanced properties such as higher strength, lighter weight, increased electrical conductivity, and chemical reactivity. Such properties allow us to address numerous issues including air pollution. Air pollution is becoming a major issue in both the developed and the developing world, and is often attributed to increased use of motor vehicles.
	How can nanotechnology help reduce air pollution? In order to reduce air pollution, modern motor vehicles are equipped with a device called *catalytic converter* that reduces emissions of three harmful compounds found in motor vehicles exhausts: • Carbon monoxide (a poisonous gas) • Nitrogen oxides (a cause of smog and acid rain) • Hydrocarbons (a cause of smog). These gases are converted into less harmful compounds (such as CO_2 and H_2O) using a catalyst.

(cont.)

Table 7.2. Lesson plan for achievement standard in Chemical Sciences (cont.)

	The catalyst used in a catalytic converter employs a combination of platinum (Pt), palladium (Pd), and rhodium (Rh), coated onto a ceramic honeycomb or ceramic beads (Figure 7.3). This is contained within a metal casing attached to the exhaust pipe, and the very fine particle size of the catalyst and the catalytic converter's honeycomb structure, provides a very large surface area where reactions take place minimizing the amount of catalyst.
Task	Produce a report that communicates your understanding of the chemistry knowledge and concepts involved in this technological application.
	In your report:
	• Describe the process and the chemistry involved • Explain how or why the chemistry applies to the application, and link your ideas to integrate the relevant chemistry with its use. This will involve elaborating, justifying, relating, evaluating, comparing and contrasting, and analyzing • Support your findings with references and/or illustrations such as photographs or diagrams.
Pedagogy	Create a Wiki page on Moodle, and establish student groups.
	Provide links to resources nanotechnology/catalytic converter: (e.g., https://en.wikipedia.org/wiki/Catalytic_converter).
	Questions posted on Wiki are:
	• What is a catalyst? • How does a catalyst work? • Name a few catalysts used in everyday life.
	Without catalytic converters, vehicles release substantial quantities of hydrocarbons, carbon monoxide, and various nitrogen oxides. These gases are a large source of ground level ozone, which causes smog and that is harmful to life. Catalytic converters are found in generators, buses, trucks, and trains; almost everything with an internal combustion engine has a form of catalytic converter attached to its exhaust system.
	A catalytic converter is a relatively simple device that uses redox reactions to reduce pollutants. It converts around 98% of the harmful fumes produced by an engine into less harmful gases. It is composed of a metal housing with a ceramic honeycomb-like interior with insulating layers. This honeycomb interior has thin wall channels that are coated with aluminum oxide. This coating is porous which increases the surface area – allowing more reactions to take place, and contains metals such as platinum, rhodium, and palladium. The converter uses oxidation and reduction reactions to convert the unwanted fumes. Recall that oxidation is the loss of electrons and that reduction is the gain of electrons. The precious metals mentioned earlier promote the transfer of electrons and, in turn, the conversion of toxic fumes.

(cont.)

CHAPTER 7

Table 7.2. Lesson plan for achievement standard in Chemical Sciences (cont.)

A three-way catalytic converter has three simultaneous functions:

Reduction of nitrogen oxides into nitrogen and oxygen:

$$NO_x \rightarrow N_x + O_x$$

The nitrogen oxides are a mixture of compounds (including NO and NO_2), and are represented generically by the formula NO_x.

Oxidation of carbon monoxide to carbon dioxide:

$$CO + \tfrac{1}{2}O_2 \rightarrow CO_2$$

Oxidation of hydrocarbons into carbon dioxide and water:

$$C_xH_{2x+2} + 2xO_2 \rightarrow xCO_2 + 2xH_2O$$

The products of this reaction also include a mixture of oxidized hydrocarbons such as alkanes, alkenes and aromatics, along with the fully oxidized products (i.e., H_2O and CO_2).

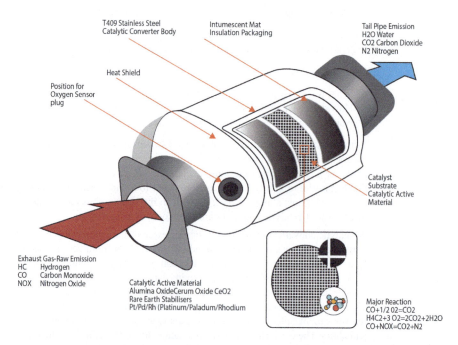

Figure 7.3. Schematic used to illustrate a catalytic converter, used as pre-visit focus before visit to the MacDiarmid Institute for Advanced Materials and Nanotechnology (produced by Sereima Raimua, graphic designer, University of the South Pacific)

Table 7.3. Pre-visit activities for achievement standard in Chemical Sciences

Students	Used school library, digital resources on Moodle, chemistry textbooks, and some New Zealand websites such as Ministry of Primary Industries, Kapuni Plant in Taranaki (Urea Production), New Zealand Institute of Chemistry, MacDiarmid Institute Victoria University of Wellington, to gain extra information. Asked parents/guardians to join LEOS as chaperones. Prepared a list of questions as a group, which were explored at the ISI. Some of these questions were used by the teacher to prepare a class worksheet. Students were allowed freedom of choice to prepare questions, some which were not formally assessed. These questions were used to prepare the class worksheet. *Class Worksheet* • What is a catalyst, and how does it work? • Why do we use catalysts in industry? • Name a few catalysts used in everyday life • What industrial processes use catalysts, and how do they work? • What happens to the catalyst if a new catalyst is invented? • What are the waste products and how are they disposed? • How does the use of catalyst affect the rate of production? [not assessed] • How does the yield get affected with and without the use of a catalyst? [not assessed] • Does the use of catalyst affect the number of staff employed at this industry? If so how? [not assessed] • How long did it take to prepare a catalyst such as the catalytic converter in cars? [not assessed] • Who funds research in nanotechnology and how to do you secure this type of funding? [not assessed]
Teachers	Assisted students to learn about both organic and inorganic/metal catalysts used in industry. Discussed different factors such as temperature, surface area, concentration and pressure that affect rate of reaction. Using energy profile diagrams, activation energy barrier was discussed, to show changes with use of catalyst. Divided students into groups they wished to work. Posted the class worksheet on Wiki, to extend discussions outside classroom hours, and moderated student posts to provide support and probe for deeper understanding.

(cont.)

CHAPTER 7

Table 7.3. Pre-visit activities for achievement standard in Chemical Sciences (cont.)

	Took students on a trip to the MacDiarmid Institute hosted at Victoria University of Wellington, New Zealand to study nanotechnology, and in particular the use of catalytic converters in new motor vehicles. Students were able to walk around the laboratory, and observe different types of machines and interact with scientists. Presentations by the scientists encouraged students to appreciate the strength of being creative and to develop inquiring mind. There was a lot of emphasis on preventing air pollution in New Zealand, which has become a national issue, with increase of cars on busy roads during peak hours of the day. Students were encouraged to record information using a recorder/smartphone as well as take photographs, which were be used in their reports.
	Contacted ISI staff to arrange the fieldtrip, and developed objectives for the visit – linking them to work completed in class.
	Prepared consent forms, informed school office and completed all required outdoor documents, student medication and first aid kit; arranged transportation, meals and parent/guardian supervisors.
	Grouped students, and provided a list of names to the ISI staff for each group, to allow them to identify individuals and communicate with different students post-visit if students needed more information or support. This list was also given to the chaperones.
	Provided class worksheet to the ISI staff before the school visit.
ISI Staff	With teachers who visited the ISI, identified safety issues, and provided information pack (downloaded from the website: https://macdiarmid.ac.nz/learning-hub/):
	Agreed on Shared Objectives of the visit. ISI staff were asked to prepare and discuss: • How can nanotechnology help reduce air pollution? • How do physical factors such as temperature, pressure, surface area, and concentration affect the way a catalytic converter operates? • Why Pd, Rh and Pt are used in preparing catalytic converters? • What is the chemistry involved in the chosen application, and explain how or why the chemistry applies to the chosen application?

Table 7.4. During-visit activities for achievement standard in Chemical Sciences

Students	Worked in groups to find answers to complete their class worksheet (Table 7.3).
	Were encouraged by teachers to approach ISI staff to seek further support, and to use other websites to help extend their knowledge.
	Recorded information using a recorder/smartphone and took photographs, used in their studies/reports. Students uploaded these images and websites on Wiki for both their teacher and feedback from other members in their group.
Teachers	Facilitated group discussions by probing student ideas, and encouraged deeper thinking: • How does nanotechnology improve standard of living of an ordinary citizen? • What would happen if we did not have catalytic converters in our modern cars? • How should hazardous waste produced during the manufacture of catalytic converter be disposed? • What could happen if they were not disposed properly?
ISI Staff	Engaged students using multimedia resources.
	Made presentations on the topic: '*How can nanotechnology improve air pollution?*,' including the MacDiarmid Institute websites, videos and realia (i.e., objects or activities used to relate classroom teaching to real life) – in this case a cut-away ceramic honey comb of a catalytic converter, metals Pd and Pt. Provided a tour of the laboratory, discussed what each stage of manufacturing involved, showed students an electron microscope, and materials for use in a catalytic converter.
	Used student list to identify students, and allowed quiet students to assist in the presentation and during group discussions. These students were asked to distribute brochures, which had web links on more information regarding nanotechnology, held ceramic honeycomb, and/or used pointers to show places or objects being discussed on the Power-Point.
	Encouraged students to ask questions.

CHAPTER 7

Table 7.5. Post-visit activities for achievement standard in Chemical Sciences

Students	Provided evidence-based arguments and explanations, to each other's postings on Wiki.
	Presented their work in class, and were quizzed by students from other groups.
	After one week, completed an assessment for two hours under examination conditions, drawing information from group pages on Wiki to complete this end-of-unit test.
Teachers	Re-visited objectives of the fieldtrip, and identified in discussion with students the types of information collected from the ISI.
	Linked student feedback to the objectives of the visit, and the assessment task.
	Placed emphasis on how chemistry is used in a selected technological application to meet the needs of society.
	Moderated student work on Moodle, to ensure they achieved the intended learning objectives for the unit.
	Marked at least five student reports, and these were subsequently moderated by peer-teachers or the Head of Department. If teacher marking agreed with that of moderator, the teacher continued to use the marking schedule and completed marking all student reports.

REFLECTIONS AND CONCLUSIONS

As can be seen from this lesson plan, this Achievement Standard required students to study, research, and demonstrate their understanding of the chemistry involved in a technological application, using a format of their choice, such as a poster, PowerPoint presentation, or written assessment. Following the description of the DIFI, we now provide some reflection we made after evaluation of the LEOS for this topic, and seek to draw some conclusions, in the same way we did for Chapter 6.

The teacher obtained feedback on the visit, evaluating findings by using student feedback from classroom discussions and postings on Wiki. Examples of student feedback included:

- Did not get the chance to see how an electron microscope operates.
- Enjoyed talking informally with ISI staff about how a converter works in old cars, and comparing this with the catalytic converter in modern vehicles.
- We had less time for lunch because some of the students had to fly out at 3.00 pm.
- Perhaps we need to have a two day trip, and stay overnight in Wellington.
- We would like to have informal conversations with these scientists about nanotechnology.

- The website provided on the day was not on their Moodle page. These were extremely helpful to search for information.
- Perhaps we could ask the scientists to prepare a video and send it to us before we visit them. This will help us prepare different types of questions.

This is helpful feedback, even if much of it relates to logistics rather than pedagogy. The teacher also considered ways of better facilitating discussions with ISI staff, so that all objectives of the visit could be addressed. Reflection on this resulted in consideration of the following:

- Identifying in advance different projects involving nanotechnology conducted by the ISI, and allowing some students choice of what they could explore when visiting the ISI. This will entail providing links to websites for these topics to the students before they visited the ISI.
- Accessing information from the website as well as the ISI staff would assist in better prepare students for the visit.
- More rigorous probing of students' ideas during group discussions at the ISI, so they could get more information from the ISI staff.

The final reflection on this LEOS was the teacher felt student's needed to have a better appreciation of chemistry as being a fundamental and enabling science that investigates molecules, the building blocks of all matter, and how they interact to affect the composition, structure and properties of substances. Molecules at macroscopic scale exhibit different properties compared to those at nanoscale, and students need to be able to see that chemistry will help us solve many future problems, including sustainable energy and food production, managing our environment, providing safe drinking water, and promoting human and environmental health. It is thus important that students are given the opportunity to familiarize themselves with a topic of their choice much earlier. This could be done by providing them with a range of topics and relevant web links. This will motivate them to explore their topic of choice more thoroughly, and mean they are better prepared to ask different questions at the ISI.

NOTE

[1] https://www.nzqa.govt.nz/ncea/subjects/chemistry/annotated-exemplars/level-1-as90931/

REFERENCE

Dalgety, J., & Coll, R. K. (2004). The influence of normative beliefs on students' enrolment choices. *Research in Science and Technological Education, 22*(1), 59–80.

CHAPTER 8

LEARNING EARTH & SPACE SCIENCES VIA LEARNING EXPERIENCES OUTSIDE SCHOOL

ABSTRACT

In this chapter lesson plans are provided for a topic related to astronomical cycles, covering the Concept, Task, and Pedagogy to be used. The topic was 'Demonstrate understanding of the effects of astronomical cycles on planet Earth', and the LEOS trip was to a planetarium. The lesson plans include details of pre-, during- and post-visit activities for teachers, students and ISI staff.

INTRODUCTION

The third learning area is Earth & Space Sciences. This is a complex area, multidisciplinary in nature, and one that is variously labelled in school curricula. The Achievement Standard used here relates understanding astronomical cycles, and focuses on what impact they have on planet Earth (Table 8.1).[1] The discussion relates to the effect of astronomical cycles on climate and weather. The activities are probably more relevant to those living in temperate climates, but given the predicted impact of climate change globally, it will be of interest to most students, wherever they live.

EARTH & SPACE SCIENCES

As with our other subject areas, Earth & Space Sciences is easy to relate to students' lives. If nothing else, the astronomical cycles affect climate and the weather, which everyone is interested in! The astronomical cycle is, however, quite complex and whilst there are various physical models that can be used in the classroom (such as the *orrery*),[2] one cannot easily see planets, or get a sense of planetary motion and important details like the tilt of the Earth. Many countries have exciting space centers and the like, which often have very powerful telescopes that allow students to view celestial bodies. Such ISIs also often have very sophisticated physical models and posters, which provide very different and valuable learning opportunities for students (Figures 8.1 & 8.2).

The Achievement Standard used here (Table 8.1), involves "demonstrating understanding of the effects of astronomical cycles on planet Earth." This requires students to demonstrate understanding of astronomical cycles, and the effects on planet Earth. *Demonstrate understanding* "involves describing astronomical cycles and the effects on planet Earth using information, visual representations, and data."

CHAPTER 8

Table 8.1. Sample achievement standard – Earth & Space Sciences

Number	AS90954	Version	1
	Achievement Standard		
Subject Reference	Science 1.15		
Title	Demonstrate understanding of the effects of astronomical cycles on planet Earth		
Level 1	Credits 4	Assessment	Internal
Subfield	Science		
Domain	Science – Core		

This achievement standard involves demonstrating understanding of the effects of astronomical cycles on planet Earth.

Achievement Criteria

Achievement	Achievement with Merit	Achievement with Excellence
Demonstrate understanding of the effects of astronomical cycles on planet Earth	Demonstrate in-depth understanding of the effects of astronomical cycles on planet Earth	Demonstrate comprehensive understanding of the effects of astronomical cycles on planet Earth

Figure 8.1. Students using a model to study phases of the Moon

LEARNING EARTH & SPACE SCIENCES VIA LEARNING EXPERIENCES

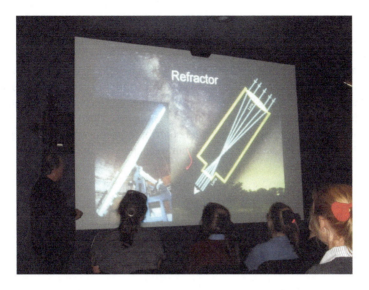

Figure 8.2. Students learning about telescopes during visit to the Planetarium

To *demonstrate in-depth understanding* "involves explaining astronomical cycles and the effects on planet Earth using information, visual representations, and data." To *demonstrate comprehensive understanding* "involves explaining thoroughly links between astronomical cycles and the effects on planet Earth using information, visual representations, and data." This may involve elaborating, applying, justifying, relating, evaluating, comparing and contrasting, or analyzing.

It is a requirement of the Achievement Standard that students choose two astronomical cycles, and investigate their effects on planet Earth:

Astronomical Cycle

- Spin of the Earth
- Orbit of Earth around Sun
- Orbit of Moon around Earth
- Effect of the Earth's tilt and the heating effect of the Sun.

Effects on Planet Earth

- Day and night
- Seasons
- Changes of temperature during the day and night
- Seasonal changes at the North and South poles, latitude of New Zealand, Tropics of Cancer and Capricorn, and the Equator
- Formation and direction of winds in the Southern hemisphere – direction of surface ocean current flows in the Pacific Ocean

CHAPTER 8

- Phases of the Moon
- Formation of tides
- Neap and Spring tides.

The Earth is tilted on its axis at 23.50°, and travels in an elliptical orbit around the Sun each year. The Earth's rotational axis – away or toward the Sun as it travels through its yearlong path around the Sun, means that summer occurs in the hemisphere tilted *toward* the Sun, and winter happens in the hemisphere tilted *away* from the Sun. The tilt of the Earth affects its angle, and contributes to the seasons and causes the daylight hours between summer and autumn to change (Figure 8.3).

Figure 8.3. Schematic illustrating the tilt of the Earth (produced by Sereima Raimua, graphic designer, University of the South Pacific)

The angle of the Sun also affects the weather patterns of the Earth. For example, hurricanes are the result of heating the oceans near the equator to over 25 °C, and forming weather cells that give rise to hurricanes. It also explains why hurricanes are seasonal. The intense heating is not a year-round event. Hurricanes begin as tropical storms over the warm moist waters of the Atlantic and Pacific Oceans near the equator. As the moisture evaporates, it rises until enormous amounts of heated moist air are twisted high in the atmosphere.

During summer, the Sun's rays hits the Earth at a steep angle because the Sun is higher in the sky (Figure 8.4). The long daylight hours during summer allows the Earth plenty of time to reach warm temperatures. This is why the days are hotter in summer. Because the Sun is higher in the sky, shadows are shorter than they are in the other three seasons. Summer is warmer and winter is colder because of the length of our days and nights. In summer, daylight lasts longer, and night is shorter.

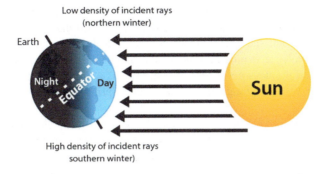

Figure 8.4. Schematic illustrating the effect the tilt of the Earth has on density of incident rays from the Sun (produced by Sereima Raimua, graphic designer, University of the South Pacific)

During winter, the Sun's rays hit the Earth at a shallow angle because the Sun is lower in the sky. These rays are spread out, minimizing the amount of energy in any given spot. The long nights and short days prevent the Earth from warming. This results in cold winters. In winter, days are shorter and nights are longer. There is more time for the Sun to warm during summer, and winter days have long cold nights.

As Earth moves in its orbit, the North Pole becomes more distant from the Sun (see top of Figure 8.5). The Sun rises lower in the sky, so the days start getting

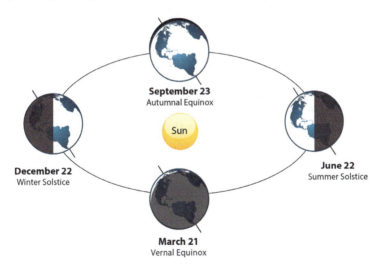

Figure 8.5. Schematic illustrating the winter/summer solstices and autumnal/vernal equinoxes (produced by Sereima Raimua, graphic designer, University of the South Pacific)

shorter in the Southern hemisphere. When the Sun is at its mid-point in the sky, the Autumn Equinox occurs (around 23 September). Day and night are both 12 hours long, and this signals the beginning of autumn. The Earth continues on its path, and the North Pole starts moving towards the Sun again. The Sun moves upwards in the skies, and the days get longer. Again, there is a midpoint when the day and night are both 12 hours long. This is called the Spring Equinox (vernal) around 21 March.

It is important to learn about the seasons because it helps children understand the passage of time, and teaches them about change. While some seasonal changes are more obvious like changes in the weather, there are many important subtle differences related to each season, like changes in the type of food that is available, types of clothes to wear, and so on. While students learn these concepts at school,

Table 8.2. Lesson plan for achievement standard in Earth & Space Sciences

This Achievement Standard involves demonstrating understanding of the effects of astronomical cycles on planet Earth.

Concept	Over the course of a year, the angle of tilt does not vary. In other words, Earth's northern axis is always pointing in the same direction in space. But the orientation of Earth's tilt with respect to the Sun, the source of light and warmth, does change as Earth orbits the Sun. This means that the Northern Hemisphere is oriented toward the Sun for half of the year, and away from the Sun for the other half. The same is true of the Southern Hemisphere.
	When the Northern Hemisphere is oriented towards the Sun, that region of Earth warms because of the corresponding increase in solar radiation. The Sun's rays strike that part of Earth at a more direct angle/low angle of incidence. This is Summer.
	When the Northern Hemisphere is oriented away from the Sun, the Sun's rays are less direct, and that part of Earth cools. This is Winter.
	Seasons in the Southern Hemisphere occur at opposite times of the year from those in the Northern Hemisphere. When the Northern Hemisphere is in summer, it is winter in the Southern Hemisphere.
	The seasons on Earth change due to the planet's angle of tilt – 23.5°, relative to the orbit around the Sun. If Earth did not tilt at all, but instead orbited exactly upright with respect to the orbit around the Sun, there would only be minor variations in temperature throughout each year as Earth moved slightly closer to the Sun and then slightly farther away. There would be temperature differences from Earth's equatorial region to the poles. But, without Earth's tilt, Earth's seasonal changes and our association of them with the various times of year would not occur. Seasons change because the angle of tilt causes the Northern and Southern Hemisphere to trade places throughout the year in receiving the Sun's light and warmth most directly.

(cont.)

Table 8.2. Lesson plan for achievement standard in Earth & Space Sciences (cont.)

Task	Students grouped to gather information, and also worked individually to process and interpret data and information, draw conclusions, and write a summary of overall findings to produce a written report. In your report demonstrate understanding of the effect of any two astronomical cycles on planet Earth from the list below: • The spin and tilt of the Earth • The orbit of the Earth around the Sun • The orbit of the Moon around the Earth • Effects of the Earth's tilt on the heating effect of the Sun. Chose one effect on planet Earth from the list below: • Day and night • Seasons • Phases of the Moon.
Pedagogy	Create a Wiki page on Moodle, and established student groups. Questions posted on Wiki are: • Describe the two terms – rotation and revolution. • Why is winter cooler than summer? • What seasons do you experience where you live? • Why do we have these seasons? *Rotation of the Earth* Demonstrated this concept by bringing a large globe into the classroom. Explained to students that Earth does spin, and then spin the globe. Placed a lamp (Power-Point projector/torch) in the middle of the classroom and turn it on. Mentioned that the lamp acts like the Sun which is always 'on' and always shining even at night. Showed students their approximate location on a world map, and taped a cotton ball, very small figurine onto the area on the globe used for demonstration. Asked two students (one quiet and one active) to help. One student held the globe while the other held the clock with hands that are easy to move. The globe was in the direct light of the lamp, or 'Sun.' This is high noon, and showed high noon on the clock. Observed how the figurine is getting most light of anywhere on the globe. Explained to the class that it will take 12 hours for the figurine to travel just halfway around. As the clock moves to 1:00, the student should move the globe a little. Did this together, hour by hour, so the class could see what was happening.

(cont.)

CHAPTER 8

Table 8.2. Lesson plan for achievement standard in Earth & Space Sciences (cont.)

By the time 6:00 was reached, the volunteer student had moved the figurine 45 degrees. Stopped at this point, so students could observe the angle of the light on the figurine. Discussed how this angle is similar to the angle of light near dusk. Observed the length shadow of the figurine, which is like the long shadows people see as evening approaches. Continued for the next six hours to midnight and stopped again. Observed there is no light on the figurine, and asked the class what they thought anyone located here on the globe would be doing at this time (Answer: Sleeping)

Continued for another six hours and asked them to take notice of how the Sun is rising on the spot on the globe with the figurine. Hour by hour, back to high noon.

Pointed out again that this demonstration showed the rotation of the Earth on its axis over the course of one day.

Revolution of the Earth Around the Sun

Discussed how while the Earth is spinning round and round, it is also moving around the Sun. Used a smaller globe, and walked around the lamp while spinning the globe.

Let students take turns holding the smaller globe, and walk around the lamp. They enjoyed using their bodies as the Earth, while walking around the lamp and spinning at the same time.

About Seasons

Earth is always moving. Every day, Earth makes one rotation on its axis. This causes day and night. Every year, Earth makes one complete orbit/revolution around the Sun. Its axis always tilts in the same direction, so the parts of Earth that receive more direct sunlight and have more daylight hours change throughout the year. This causes seasons; that is, times of the year with particular patterns of weather and daylight, which vary depending on where people live. Most places experience four seasons: Spring, summer, autumn, and winter.

Sun's Path in the Sky

Every day, the Sun appears to move across the sky from East to West because of Earth's rotation.

When the Sun's position is higher in the sky at noon, there are more hours of daylight, and sunlight strikes the surface at a more vertical angle. The higher the Sun appears in the sky, the more solar energy reaches the surface. In general, this makes it warmer.

(cont.)

Table 8.2. Lesson plan for achievement standard in Earth & Space Sciences (cont.)

When the Sun appears lower at noon, there are fewer hours of daylight, and, since sunlight strikes less directly, less energy reaches the surface.

The equinoxes are the only two days of the year when the Sun rises due east and sets due west.

Seasonal Lag

Earth receives energy from sunlight and loses energy to space. A location's temperature will go up or down based on the balance of incoming and outgoing energy.

As daylight hours increase at a location, the oceans, land, and atmosphere receive more energy and lose less energy.

A location receives the most energy on the summer solstice, but it continues to receive more energy than it loses for several weeks after the solstice, temperatures continue to get warmer. The warmest temperatures for a location usually occur several weeks after the summer solstice.

Similarly, the coldest temperatures for a location are usually several weeks after the winter solstice.

Earth's Orbit

Earth's orbit is not a perfect circle, it is elliptical, but Earth's varying distance from the Sun is not the only cause of the seasons. Compared with how far away the Sun is, the change in Earth's distance throughout the year does not make much difference.

Table 8.3. Pre-visit activities for achievement standard in Earth & Space Sciences

Students	Used school library, digital resources on Moodle, and Astronomy/Science textbooks and other websites such as Auckland Astronomical Society, Wellington Astronomical Society, University of Canterbury Mt John Observatory, Stardome Observatory, to obtain additional information.
	Asked parents/guardians and elders to join LEOS to act as chaperones.
	Prepared a list of questions as a group, which were explored at the ISI. Some of these questions were used by the teacher to prepare a class worksheet. Students were allowed freedom of choice to prepare questions, some which were not formally assessed. These questions were used to prepare the class worksheet.

(cont.)

CHAPTER 8

Table 8.3. Pre-visit activities for achievement standard in Earth & Space Sciences (cont.)

	Class Worksheet • How does the angle of the Sun affect the amount of heat received by the Earth? • What are the causes of tides on the Earth? • How do the phases of the Moon affect the Earth? • How does the angle of incidence compare between morning and midday? Between morning and evening? • What role do you think the angle of incidence plays in determining seasons? • What role does the distance between the Sun and Earth play in determining seasons? • Describe summer solstice and winter solstice? • Describe autumnal and vernal equinox? • What are some examples of seasonal changes in the environment? • Do all locations on Earth experience the same kinds of seasons? • How do seasonal changes affect plants and animals? • If you compared the angle of incidence at midday during winter and summer, which season would have a higher angle of incidence? Why? • What kind of data could you gather if you wanted to study seasonal changes? [not assessed] • What would happen to the seasons if the tilt were less than 23.5°? [not assessed] • What would happen if it was greater than 23.5°? [not assessed] • What type of qualification do you need to work as an educator in an observatory? [not assessed].
Teachers	Described why we have four seasons. Noting we have seasons because the Earth is tilted as it makes its yearly journey around the Sun. The Earth's axis is tilted at an angle of 23.5°. This means that the Earth is always 'pointing' to one side as it goes around the Sun. So, sometimes the Sun is in the direction that the Earth is pointing, but not at other times. The varying amounts of sunlight around the Earth during the year, creates the seasons. The tilt of the Earth's axis is the most important reason why seasons occur. There are hot summers and cold winters because of the tilt of the Earth's axis. The tilt of the Earth means that the Earth will lean towards the Sun (summer), or lean away from the Sun (winter), 6 months later. In between these spring and autumn occur. *Important Facts:* • The Earth revolves around the Sun • The North pole always points the same way as the Earth revolves around the Sun • The Earth movement around the Sun causes seasons. Divided students into groups they wished to work with, to discuss the class worksheet.

(cont.)

Table 8.3. Pre-visit activities for achievement standard in Earth & Space Sciences (cont.)

	Posted the class worksheet on Wiki, to extend discussions outside classroom hours. Teachers moderated these posts to provide support and probe for deeper understanding.
	Contacted the ISI staff to arrange the trip. Upon confirmation, informed students about this, and started developing objectives for the visit by linking them to work completed in class.
	Took students on a trip to an observatory to study links between astronomical cycles and the effects on planet Earth.
	Ensured students at the observatory listened to the presentation to learn about basic astronomy and telescopes.
	In the dome shaped planetarium, ensured students observed the Milky Way, and learned the basics of navigating the night sky using points of reference such as Polaris (North Star) and various constellations. There were also computer generated images of other planets, nebulae, and distant galaxies which students could see close up.
	Ensured students moved into the observatory room to explore different parts of a large telescope. Because the visit was during the daytime, the ISI staff put a sunfilter on the lens to show students how it worked. Students took turns and could see the Moon through the telescope.
	Encouraged students to take images of the Moon using cameras and cellphones through the telescope.
	Prepared consent forms, informed school office and completed all required fieldtrip documents, student medication and first aid kit; arranged transportation, meals and parent/guardian supervisors.
	Grouped students, and provided a list of names to the ISI staff for each group, to allow them to identify individuals and communicate with different students post-visit if students needed more information or support. This list was also given to the chaperones.
	Provided class worksheet including student names to the ISI staff before the school visit.
ISI Staff	With teachers who visited the ISI, identified safety related issues, and collected information pack (download from the ISI website: https://www.stardome.org.nz/education-school-trips/).
	Encouraged students to record information using a recorder/smartphone, and to take photographs to be used in their studies.
	Agreed on the Shared Objectives of the visit. ISI staff were asked to prepare and discuss:

(cont.)

CHAPTER 8

Table 8.3. Pre-visit activities for achievement standard in Earth & Space Sciences (cont.)

Astronomical Cycles • Spin of the Earth • Orbit of Earth around Sun • Orbit of Moon around Earth • Effect of the Earth's tilt, and the heating effect of the Sun. *Effects on Planet Earth* • Day and Night • Seasons • Seasonal changes at the North and South poles, latitude of New Zealand, Tropics of Cancer and Capricorn, and the Equator • Phases of the Moon.

Table 8.4. During-visit activities for achievement standard in Earth & Space Sciences

Students	Worked in groups to find answers to complete class worksheet (Table 8.3). Were encouraged by teachers to approach ISI staff to seek further support, and use other websites to help extend their knowledge. Recorded information using a recorder/smartphone, and took photographs, which were used in their studies/reports. Students uploaded these images and websites on Wiki for both their teacher and feedback from other members in their group.
Teachers	Facilitated group discussions by probing student ideas, and encouraged deeper thinking, using the following questions: • Does the desert get hotter than forest during the day – if so, why? • Why do settlements around water bodies such as the sea experience less change in ambient temperature? • Does the Moon also rotate on its axis, or do we see only one side of the Moon? • What forces if any attracts the three celestial bodies in their orbits? • Why are certain parts of the planet showing extreme temperature changes than others? • Does the Moon experience seasons also?
ISI Staff	Engaged students using multimedia resources. Prepared presentations on the topic: *Astronomical cycles and effects on planet Earth*, and *Seasons and Phases of the Moon*. The presentation included websites, videos and realia (i.e., objects or activities used for classroom teaching) – in this case models of how students could create different phases of the Moon using a shoebox, table tennis ball, and a torch. The presentations used Power-Point, videos and a dome in the planetarium to project images.

(cont.)

Table 8.4. During-visit activities for achievement standard in Earth & Space Sciences (cont.)

	Students were divided into two groups with two ISI staff in each. While one group visited the planetarium, the other was guided through the exhibition gallery, and provided with a hands-on tutorial session in a multimedia room. Each group took turn to visit the room where a telescope was used to view the Moon.
	A student list was used to identify students who had some knowledge about constellations, seasonal changes, phases of the Moon, and formation and types of tides. Quiet students assisted during presentation and recording of information during group discussions, and assisted ISI staff in demonstrating different phases of the Moon using the model, distributed brochures which had web links on more information regarding seasonal and information on tides. Used pointers to measure the angle of incidence and length of the shadow, for different times of the day.
	Encouraged students to ask questions.

Table 8.5. Post-visit activities for achievement standard in Earth & Space Sciences

Students	Uploaded photos and explanations to the questions they had composed for the visit. They also helped answer each other's questions, when more explanation was needed.
	Recorded information which was useful in writing reports.
	One week after the trip, completed an assessment for two hours under examination conditions, using information from classroom sessions, and group pages on Wiki.
Teachers	Revisited the objectives of the visit, and used questions from the worksheet to develop deeper understanding of the topic. Allowed students to take turns in presenting their findings to the class using Power-Point.
	Placed emphasis on how three celestial bodies interacted to create seasons, tides, and different phases of the Moon.
	Marked at least five student reports, and these were subsequently moderated by peer-teachers or the Head of Department. If teacher marking agreed with that of moderator, the teacher continued to use the marking schedule and completed marking all student reports.

it is helpful if they visit sites where they can both observe as well as learn from specialists such as ISI staff at an observatory.

This subject is quite complex and multifaceted. So there is more detail provided in the tables than for the previous two topics in earlier chapters.

CHAPTER 8

REFLECTIONS AND CONCLUSIONS

As mentioned earlier, this is a complex and demanding topic, with many abstract and difficult ideas. As with earlier chapters, we now look at the implementation of the DIFI, and reflect on feedback for improvement.

This Achievement Standard required students to demonstrate understanding of the effect of astronomical cycles on planet Earth. The use of LEOS helped enormously in student understanding, as it opened students to sophisticated displays and equipment few schools could provide. The exposure to fabulous equipment like telescopes was exciting and inspiring to students. The LEOS provided them with opportunities to engage in activities such as astronomical observations, and/or modelling through the use of 3D models, animations, and visiting the Observatory. The planetarium provided a dark room with a dome shaped roof to help students learn about 88 constellations, satellites and their functions, seasonal changes due to the movement of three celestial bodies, and the differences between an astronaut and an astronomer.

These were highly valuable learning experiences and allowed students to independently research information using the Internet on:

- Specific astronomical cycle (or cycles) and its effects on planet Earth
- Reasons for the effects on the Earth of the relevant astronomical cycles;
- The interrelationship of the different astronomical cycles – the links between these cycles, and the links with their effects on planet Earth, and
- Relevant images and processed/interpreted data as well as text that explained their findings and conclusions.

The LEOS stimulated considerable interest in this area of Earth & Space Sciences, and it was this that led to students' interest in researching additional topics.

Information regarding the learning of this topic was obtained from feedback sheet of the ISI, which covered preparations conducted in collaboration with the school and teachers. Additionally, students used evaluation sheet to provide feedback to the ISI staff. Copies of this feedback were also used by teachers to evaluate their teaching and learning. Evaluating comments on Wiki both before and after the visit, was an effective way to measure students learning and depth of understanding. This was evident from the addition of different website links students provided to each other in their groups, responses to each other's inquiries, and questions posed to their teachers to seek further clarification.

This feedback indicated that students enjoyed visiting the ISI because they could experience a different learning environment inside the planetarium which increased their curiosity, and made learning more fun and enjoyable. They liked using models to learn about phases of the Moon and having the opportunity to make inquiries with an 'expert' was equally rewarding. A major highlight was to view the Moon using a *real* telescope, and take images using their camera. Some of these images were uploaded on Wiki sites for students to view and discuss.

Specific feedback from students was:

- Showing movies followed by classroom-based presentation helped us learn how these three celestial bodies interact, especially eight phases of the Moon
- Learning about how telescopes are used to view objects beyond Earth
- Learning how the Sun, Earth and Moon interact to create seasons, day, night, month and year.

The teachers considered ways of improving plans for taking learning outside school. The teachers found team teaching was necessary, because not all teachers had adequate level of experience in teaching about formation of tides, formation and the direction of winds in the southern hemisphere, and direction of surface ocean current flows in the Pacific Ocean. However, they had enough knowledge on seasonal changes, day and night and phases on the Moon. This was one of the reasons why they had not included these three effects of Earth when planning for LEOS. However, teachers reported when evaluating student's feedback, it was apparent that there were some students who were interested in learning about how astronomical cycles brought about these three effects on planet Earth. Teachers also felt to provide diversity in the topic, Māori legends taught in earlier school days could be shared by inviting Kaumātua (i.e., Māori elders) to school, to discuss Matariki.[3] This they felt would help motivate students to explore their topic of choice, and be prepared to ask different types of questions at the ISI, which would be useful when linking legends and myths with scientific reasoning.

NOTES

[1] https://www.nzqa.govt.nz/ncea/subjects/science/annotated-exemplars/level-1-as90954/
[2] See https://www.youtube.com/watch?v=aN3VLcqs3MI
[3] Matariki is the Māori name for the cluster of stars also known as the Pleiades. It rises in mid-winter and for many Māori, it heralds the start of a new year.

CHAPTER 9

LEARNING PHYSICAL SCIENCES VIA LEARNING EXPERIENCES OUTSIDE SCHOOL

ABSTRACT

In this chapter lesson plans are provided for a topic related to heat and insulation, covering the Concept, Task, and Pedagogy to be used. The topic was 'Investigating implications of heat for everyday life', and the LEOS trip was to a modern show home. The lesson plans include details of pre-, during- and post-visit activities for teachers, students and ISI staff.

INTRODUCTION

As mentioned in earlier chapters of Part 2, the learning areas are somewhat arbitrarily labeled, based on broad, often multidisciplinary terms. The title used for this chapter is *Physical Sciences*, which broadly includes subjects labeled more traditionally 'physics' (and related areas), but not the Chemical Sciences (which are covered in Chapter 7). Teachers should, as with the other chapters, look to where the subject matter here fits into their own curriculum/learning areas.

Consistent with the theme of trying to choose topics and LEOS experiences that relate to students' everyday lives, here 'energy' is the topic of study. For temperate climates in particular, such a topic relates easily to everyday life, especially in cold winter months when many families consider how to heat their homes without undue cost. The Achievement Standard used here involves investigating implications of heat for everyday life (Table 9.1).[1]

PHYSICAL SCIENCES

Energy is one of the most important topics in the Physical Sciences, because so many processes are governed by energy considerations. There is often confusion about the term, and careless use of the term interchangeably with other related terms such as heat, work, and effort.

As with the other Achievement Standards, there are guidelines provided for the different levels of achievement. To *investigate*, "involves showing awareness of how science is involved in an issue that students encounter in their everyday lives. This requires at least one of the following:

CHAPTER 9

Table 9.1. Sample achievement standard – Physical sciences

Number	AS90943	Version	1
	Achievement Standard		
Subject Reference	Science 1.4		
Title	Investigating implications of heat for everyday life.		
Level 1	Credits 4	Assessment	Internal
Subfield	Science		
Domain	Science – Core		

This achievement standard involves demonstrating understanding of the effects of astronomical cycles on planet Earth.

Achievement Criteria

Achievement	Achievement with Merit	Achievement with Excellence
Investigate implications of heat for everyday life.	Investigate, in depth, implications of heat for everyday life.	Investigate, comprehensively, implications of heat for everyday life.

- the collection of primary evidence from an investigation, and relating it to the scientific theory relevant to the issue;
- the collection of secondary data, and identification of scientific theory relevant to the issue under investigation. The issue must involve two different views, positions, perspectives, arguments, explanations, or opinions."

Similarly, to *investigate in-depth*, "involves providing reasons for the way science is involved in this issue. This requires at least one of the following:

- the collection of primary evidence from an investigation and relating it to the scientific theory relevant to the issue in order to give an explanation of the issue being investigated
- the collection of sufficient relevant secondary data and the application of the identified scientific theory relevant to the issue to explain the different views, positions, perspectives, arguments, explanations, or opinions of the issue under investigation."

Finally, to *investigate comprehensively*, "providing reasons and linking them in a way that clearly explains the science that is involved in this issue. This requires at least one of the following:

- the collection of primary evidence from an investigation and relating it to the scientific theory relevant to the issue in order to give a comprehensive and critical explanation of the issue being investigated

- the collection of sufficient relevant secondary data and the application of the identified scientific theory relevant to the issue to critically evaluate the different views, positions, perspectives, arguments, explanations, or opinions of the issue under investigation."

The Achievement Standard also notes that "aspects of heat may be chosen from, but are not limited to temperature, heat energy, specific heat capacity, conduction, convection, radiation, insulation, phase changes, latent heat, the relationships that are relevant to the investigation."

Many homes in temperate climates such as New Zealand, lack sufficient insulation. People who live in poorly insulated homes either live in a cold, damp home or use substantial amounts of energy for heating, at great cost. Two methods of reducing heat loss are to use fiberglass pads or polystyrene sheets under floorboards, in wall cavities, or in ceiling spaces. In a house, heat escapes through the walls, roof, floor, windows and doors, and this is exacerbated in poorly insulated homes (Figure 9.1). By insulating a house and keeping the heat in for longer, the energy needed to heat it, and the fuel bill is greatly reduced, up to by half. If the design and building materials of the house are optimized, the Sun's energy can be utilized to heat the house. Energy efficient house plans can greatly reduce energy costs for the life of the house. Students may be under the impression that Energy Star[2] heating ratings for appliances and cooling systems make an energy efficient house. However, house design decisions such as site orientation, ventilation, and balancing solar loads and construction design make a far greater impact on energy use. Conservation of energy also can help to lessen pollution and reduce greenhouse gas emissions. While

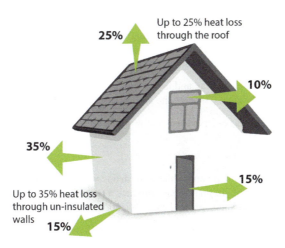

Figure 9.1. Schematic showing heat loss from a home (produced by Sereima Raimua, graphic designer, University of the South Pacific)

CHAPTER 9

Table 9.2. Lesson plan for achievement standard in Physical Sciences

	This Achievement Standard involves investigating the implications of heat for everyday life.
Concept	Heat transfer occurs in a number of ways, such as thermal conduction, thermal convection, and thermal radiation. When an object is at a different temperature from another or its surroundings, heat flows so the body and the surroundings reach the same temperature, at which point they are in thermal equilibrium. Such spontaneous heat transfer always occurs from a region of high temperature to another region of lower temperature, as described in the second law of thermodynamics. Metals are good conductors of heat.
	A well-insulated home is warmer in winter and cooler in summer. This is because a good insulation material and home design keep heat in, and retains heat for a long time.[3] Common insulation materials used in homes and other buildings are:
	<ul><li>Fiberglass – the most common insulation used in modern times. Because of how it is made by effectively weaving fine strands of glass into an insulation material, fiberglass is able to minimize heat transfer. Fiberglass is an excellent non-flammable insulation material, with R-values ranging from R-2.9 to R-3.8 per inch</li><li>Mineral Wool – refers to several different types of insulation. First, it may refer to glass wool which is fiberglass manufactured from recycled glass. Mineral wool can be purchased in sections or as a loose material. Most mineral wool does not contain fire resistant additives, making it unsuitable for use in situations where extreme heat is likely. However, it is not combustible, and when used in conjunction with other, more fire resistant forms of insulation, it can be an effective way of insulating large areas. Mineral wool has a R-values ranging from R-2.8 to R-3.5</li><li>Cellulose Insulation Material – has R-values between R-3.1 and R-3.7. Recent studies on cellulose shown that it is good for use in minimizing fire damage.</li></ul>
	What type of designing and layout of a house is best for keeping it warm? In other words, what will keep the home cooler in summer and warmer in winter?
	In a house, heat escapes through the walls, roof, floor, windows and doors (Figure 9.1).
Task	*Part One: Designing the House (Pairs)*
	Imagine that you are an architect (someone who designs houses), and design your own home. In your report, produce a floor-plan (for a single level home) of your home, and consider heat implications of the home you have designed.
	Part Two: What to build the home out of, and how to insulate (Individual Report)
	Now that you have designed your home, decide what to build it out of, and how to best insulate it.

(cont.)

Table 9.2. Lesson plan for achievement standard in Physical Sciences (cont.)

Pedagogy	Create a Wiki page on Moodle, and establish student groups. Provide links to resources on R-values.

Questions posted on Wiki are:
- Name a few insulators used in everyday life
- How does an insulator work?
- What does R-value mean?
- Why is it important to consider R-value when designing home?

Insulation, or more correctly thermal insulation, is a general term used to describe products that reduce heat loss or heat gain by providing a barrier between areas that are significantly different in temperature. There are a number of items in homes that benefit from insulation – such as central heating boilers and hot water pipes. However buildings themselves can be made more energy efficient by careful orientation to the Sun, and by insulation. Home insulation reduces the amount of heat that escapes from a building in the winter, and protects it from getting too warm in the summer.

Air is a poor conductor of heat, so tiny pockets of air trapped in insulation minimize the amount of heat that can pass between the inside and outside of a house.

This means that in winter, the heat stays inside a home, and in the summer it stays outside.

Different types of insulation materials have different properties, so are suitable for different areas of a building.

Glass and mineral wool are versatile insulation materials which can be used in a wide range of buildings, including commercial buildings such as shops and offices; public buildings such as schools and hospitals; and residential houses and flats. In residential buildings, there are three main areas where insulation is needed; walls, roof and floors.

Wall Insulation
The walls of a home represent the largest surface through which heat can escape, and are consequently responsible for around 60 per cent of the heat lost from an uninsulated house. This breaks down to about 35 per cent escaping through the walls, 15 per cent through the doors, and 10 per cent via the windows.

Roof Insulation
Heat rises, causing a further 25 per cent of heat energy to escape through an uninsulated roof. Installing roof insulation is one of the most cost effective ways of improving the energy efficiency of a home, and it can be done without professional help in around 2–3 hours. The Government's recommended minimum depth of insulation is 270 mm, however, many homes have much less than this.

Floor Insulation
Insulation is used in ground floors for thermal insulation, and in intermediate floors for thermal and acoustic insulation.

CHAPTER 9

Figure 9.2. Teacher facilitating discussions between students and ISI staff at the show home

Figure 9.3. Students working in pairs at the show home

Table 9.3. Pre-visit activities for achievement standard in Physical Sciences

Students	Used school library, digital resources on Moodle, and Physics textbooks to find information, and other New Zealand websites such as Pink Batts, Genesis Energy, New Zealand (a local energy provider), Stonewood Homes and Generation Development (local home construction companies), to gain extra information.
	Asked parents/guardians and elders to join LEOS as chaperones.
	Prepared a list of questions as a group, which were explored at the ISI. Some of these questions were used by the teacher to prepare a class worksheet. Students were allowed freedom of choice to prepare questions, some which were not formally assessed. These questions were used to prepare the class worksheet.
	Class Worksheet <ul><li>What is an insulator, and how does it work?</li><li>Why do we use different types of insulation in the building industry?</li><li>Name a few insulators used in everyday life</li><li>What industrial processes use insulators, and how do they work?</li><li>Besides the thickness of insulating material, what other factors affect heat travel?</li><li>What happens to the insulators when the house gets older?</li><li>How does the house prices compare with and without much insulation? [not assessed]</li><li>What type of training is needed to build a well-insulated home? [not assessed]</li><li>How long does it take for insulators to stop working effectively? [not assessed]</li><li>How much money can we save during winter for a well-insulated 4-bedroom home? [not assessed]</li><li>What are the waste products of producing insulators, and how are they disposed? [not assessed]</li></ul>
Teachers	Assisted students to learn about three different ways by which heat travels, namely convection, conduction and radiation. Also, discussed insulation to help identify air particles between the two surfaces, help to avoid heat transfer, since the particles are far apart. Also, discussed different factors such as surface area, and R-value, which affect the rate of heat travel. R-value is a measure of resistance to heat flow through a given thickness of material. In theory, the higher the R-value, the greater resistance. But this is one of four key factors that determine effectiveness of an insulating material.
	Divided students into groups they wished to work with, to prepare questions for the class worksheet.
	Posted class worksheet on Wiki, to extend discussions outside classroom hours. Teachers moderated these posts to provide support and probe for deeper understanding.

(cont.)

CHAPTER 9

Table 9.3. Pre-visit activities for achievement standard in Physical Sciences (cont.)

	Took students on a trip to a Show Home, a modern designed house to study designing of a house, learn types of materials used, and particularly insulating materials used in building. Allowed students to walk both inside and outside the house to study the layout of the building in a given space, orientation of the house towards the Sun, types and sizes of rooms, which rooms to be kept warm, direction of sunrise and sunset, and which rooms gets the most sunshine. Also, to become aware of the building code regulations such as:

- The bathroom/toilet entrances cannot be near the kitchen entrance.
- Each room must have an opening window (except walk in robes/closets).
- Access to certain rooms cannot be via bedrooms (e.g. to get to the kitchen you cannot go through the bedroom).

Provided an opportunity for students to learn and ask questions to the designers and architects. Demonstrations by ISI staff showing different types of insulating materials for building and showing a number of house designs provided an enriching learning experience. There was a lot of emphasis on saving cost of keeping homes warm, and subsequently preventing people from getting sick.

Encouraged students to record information using a recorder/smartphone as well as take photographs, which will be used in their studies.

Contacted the ISI staff to arrange the fieldtrip. Upon confirmation, teachers informed students about this, and started developing objectives for the visit by linking them to work completed in class.

Prepared consent forms, informed school office and completed all required outdoor documents, student medication and first aid kit; arranged transportation, meals and parent/guardian supervisors.

Grouped students, and provided a name list to the ISI staff for each group, to allow them to identify individuals and communicate with different students post-visit if students needed more information or support. This list was also given to the chaperones.

Provided class worksheet to ISI staff before the school visit.

ISI Staff	With teachers who visited the ISI, identified safety related issues, and provided ISI information pack (downloaded from the ISI website, https://www.generation.co.nz/).

Agreed on Shared Objectives for the visit. ISI staff were asked to prepare and discuss the following:
- Say what factors are considered when designing a floor plan
- Share a number of floor plans and discuss the designs with students
- Show how to select types of insulation needed for the different parts of the house

(cont.)

Table 9.3. Pre-visit activities for achievement standard in Physical Sciences (cont.)

- Say what factors are used when calculating R-value for insulation materials
- Explain how does an insulator work in the three key parts of the house – floor, wall, and roof
- Show fiberglass, polystyrene and Pink Batts[4] and discuss the insulation ability of each material, and how they compare with each other
- Provide a scientific description of how physical properties of materials affect their ability to insulate (prevent heat loss)
- Explain why one material was a more efficient insulator than the other
- Describe how heat is lost in a typical home
- Explain why heat loss should be prevented in a home.

Table 9.4. During-visit activities for achievement standard in Physical Sciences

Students	Worked in groups to find answers to complete the class worksheet (Table 9.3).
	Were encouraged by teachers to approach ISI staff to seek further support, and use other websites to help extend their knowledge.
	Recorded information using a recorder/smartphone, and took photographs, which were used in their studies/reports. Students uploaded these images and websites on Wiki for both their teacher and feedback from other members in their group.
Teachers	Facilitated group discussions by probing student ideas, and encouraged deeper thinking: • What type of insulation is used in interior walls? • What types of insulation is used in the ceiling and why? • How should hazardous waste produced during the manufacture of insulators be disposed? • What could happen if they were not disposed properly? • What happens to insulation over a period of time? • How does polyurethane foam compare with Styrofoam?
ISI Staff	Engaged students using multimedia resources (a group of three ISI staff – Architect, Designer and Builder, addressed the students, and also facilitated group discussions).
	Prepared presentations on the topic: *What type of designing and layout of a house is best for keeping your home warm?* The presentation included websites, videos and realia (i.e., objects or activities used to relate classroom teaching to real life) – in this case, floor plans of a number of both single and double story houses, models of houses, Pink Batts, tinted glasses, Styrofoam, joists, roof structure showing how Pink Batts are arranged around the ceiling, water tanks in the ceiling, and a tour of the Show Home.

(cont.)

Table 9.4. During-visit activities for achievement standard in Physical Sciences (cont.)

> Discussed how the house was designed to receive maximum sunlight, and types of insulation used, including those inside such as wool carpet.
>
> Used student list to identify students who had some experience in building homes, and parents who had similar experience. The quiet students assisted in the presentation, and during group discussions. These students were asked to distribute brochures, which had web links on more information regarding R-values and building materials, copies of floor plans for houses (e.g., https://stonewood.co.nz/home-designs/), and/or used pointers to show parts of the models of houses.
>
> Encouraged students to ask questions.

Table 9.5. Post-visit activities for achievement standard in Physical Sciences

Students	Provided evidence-based arguments and explanations to each other's postings on Wiki. Uploaded pictures of building materials taken at the ISI, which helped extend discussions mainly on the importance of R-values.
	Presented their work in class, and were quizzed by students from other groups. Shared designs of floor plans on home insulation. The differences in their presentations were the style of a single-story home. Some also added gardens and patios to their plans. Student presentations had a strong emphasis on types of materials used, R-vales of these building materials, how will they help to insulate their homes.
	After a week, students completed an assessment for two hours under examination conditions, using information from classroom sessions, and group pages on Wiki to complete this end-of-unit test.
Teachers	Re-visited the objectives of the fieldtrip, and identified types of information collected from the ISI. Emphasis was placed on insulating ability of each material, scientific description of how the physical properties of materials affect their ability to insulate (prevent heat loss), linked the data students have gathered to scientific theory, for example by providing scientific reasons why one material was a more efficient insulator than the other. Described how heat is lost in a typical home, and explained why heat loss should be prevented.
	Moderated student work on Moodle, to ensure they achieved the intended learning objectives for the unit.
	Marked at least five student reports, and these were subsequently moderated by peer-teachers or the Head of Department. If teacher marking agreed with that of moderator, the teacher continued to use the marking schedule and completed marking all student reports.

students learn these concepts at school, it is helpful if they are able to visit sites where they can both observe as well as learn from specialists such as house designers and architects about designing a floor plan, which is heating efficient. The LEOS for this Achievement Standard involved visiting a modern Show Home, which took energy into consideration during planning and construction (Figures 9.2 & 9.3).

REFLECTIONS AND CONCLUSIONS

This Achievement Standard requires students to show awareness of heat impact on everyday life. The context for this assessment task is an investigation of the effectiveness of insulating houses. Learning was facilitated by a visit to a modern Show Home that exemplified energy-conscious design. The assessment dealt with interesting and valuable science concepts such as heat transfer, which required prior knowledge of conduction, radiation, convection, and temperature as a measure of heat energy. The Show Home provided an ideal environment for such topics, and conducting a visit during winter months meant the science learning was very topical.

The teacher obtained feedback on the visit, evaluating findings by using student feedback from classroom discussions, and postings on Wiki. Examples of student feedback included:

- Enjoyed seeing how Pink Batts are put around the joist in the floor, and the hot water tanks in the ceiling
- The architect provided floor plans for 15 single-story houses
- It was interesting how the cost varies for each one even though the floor size is the same
- Demonstrating building materials like Pink Batts, Styrofoam, and double-glazed glasses, and using R-values to make comparisons, and explaining why they were used in the different parts of house was truly exciting
- I learnt about the importance of R-value more from the architect than what I did during my Physics lessons
- Perhaps we could invite one of the ISI staff to visit us in school post-visit, and help answer any other questions we have
- It will be good to have some of these building materials in our laboratory also
- It would have been good if the ISI staff could compare the design of an old home with a modern home, and explain to us on improvements in home design.

The teacher also considered ways of better facilitating discussions with ISI staff, so that all objectives of the visit could be thoroughly covered. Here ideas included:

- Students could be asked to bring their own home floor plans, and discuss how to improve heat insulation
- They could also be asked to bring floor plans for an old and a new home to compare

CHAPTER 9

- Providing more website links on the Moodle page to provide more information, and better prepare students for the visit.

One issue raised by teachers related to the importance of R-values; something most students were unfamiliar with before the LEOS. Teachers felt that it was important to place more emphasis on teaching students about R-value and its importance to the building industry, prior to the visit. As noted above, an R-value is a measure of how well an object, per unit of its exposed area, resists conductive flow of heat. The greater the R-value, the greater the resistance, and so the better the thermal insulating properties of the object. R-values are used in describing effectiveness of insulation and in analysis of heat flow across assemblies (such as walls, roofs, and windows) under steady-state conditions. Heat flow through an object is driven by temperature difference between two sides of the object, and the R-value quantifies how effectively the object resists this drive. Moreover, as long as the materials involved are dense solids in direct mutual contact, R-values are additive; for example, the total R-value of an object composed of several layers of material is the sum of the R-values of the individual layers.

The final reflection on this LEOS is that it is important students bring a floor plan of their choice for discussion in the classroom, and to provide diversity of topics and relevant web links. This will help motivate them to explore their topic of choice more thoroughly, and be prepared to ask different types of questions at the ISI, which will assist them in learning the topic better.

NOTES

[1] https://www.nzqa.govt.nz/ncea/subjects/science/annotated-exemplars/level-1-as90943/
[2] See https://www.energywise.govt.nz/energy-labels/energy-rating-labels/
[3] Often this is described using 'R-values' see https://www.building.govt.nz/building-code-compliance/h-energy-efficiency/h1-energy-efficiency/building-code-requirements-for-house-insulation/r-values-for-common-construction-types/
[4] A common New Zealand home insulation material, see https://pinkbatts.co.nz/

APPENDIX

THE NEW ZEALAND CURRICULUM AND SCIENCE CURRICULUM

New Zealand has two curriculum documents, The *New Zealand Curriculum* (http://nzcurriculum.tki.org.nz/The-New-Zealand-Curriculum), and the Māori language version *Te Marautanga o Aotearoa* (http://tmoa.tki.org.nz/). According to the Ministry, the Curriculum is a "clear statement of what is deemed important in education in New Zealand. The Curriculum provides *Directions for Learning* and a *Vision* of "Young people who will be confident, connected, actively involved, lifelong learners" (MoE, 2007, p. 7). The Curriculum specifies *Values* (Excellence; Innovation, Inquiry & Curiosity; Diversity; Equity; Community & Participation; Ecological Sustainability; Integrity; Respect), *Key Competences* (Thinking; Using Language, Symbols & Texts; Managing Self; Relation to Others; Participating & Contributing), and *Learning Areas* (English; The Arts; Health & Physical Education; Learning Languages; Mathematics & Statistics; Science; Social Sciences; Technology). Teachers are expected to use the Curriculum to develop a school curriculum, suited to their own circumstances and environment.

The Science Curriculum (http://nzcurriculum.tki.org.nz/The-New-Zealand-Curriculum/Science/) spans eight levels, and is described in sets of *Achievement Objectives* (http://nzcurriculum.tki.org.nz/The-New-Zealand-Curriculum/Science/Achievement-objectives); these in turn are organized within *Learning Strands* (http://nzcurriculum.tki.org.nz/The-New-Zealand-Curriculum/Science/Learning-area-structure). There are two groups of learning strands; *Contextual Strands*, and *Integrating Strands*. The former, is made up of four strands: *Living World*, *Physical World*, *Material World*, and *Planet Earth and Beyond*. Integrating strands include overarching ideas such as *Nature of Science*. Each strand is divided into eight levels, which detail the progression of the science curriculum from junior to senior secondary levels.

A number of achievement objectives are described in each strand and at each level. At each level, the achievement objective describes the expected learning in science. For Levels 1–5 (7–14 years old), the achievement objectives are linked, on average, to a two year period of learning; for Levels 6, 7 and 8 (NCEA Levels 1, 2 & 3 for students aged 15–17 years), the objectives are linked to a one year period of learning.

The Curriculum encourages teachers to link achievement objectives from different strands to provide integrated learning experiences. This allows schools to prepare

APPENDIX

their own school science scheme. It is intended that the school science scheme sets specific learning outcomes, which are derived from achievement objectives as this provides the learning criteria, and which is used to structure the learning experiences for students. Although the learning objectives can be prescriptive, the learning contexts, possible learning experiences and assessment types should allow flexibility in how the aims and objectives can be fulfilled. So what will be common across all schools in New Zealand, is their science schemes will target the attainment of the same achievement objectives, but they will (and indeed should) use different contexts and learning experiences, as well as different formative assessment regimes, to attain the learning described by these achievement objectives.

The Curriculum also identifies teaching approaches that the Ministry say have a positive impact on student learning including:

- *Facilitating Shared Learning*: This is where the students learn as they engage in shared activities and conversations with other people such as family members, their group members, in this case ISI staff and people in the wider community. This allows students to engage in a reflective discourse with others and build the language, science jargon, they need in order to take their learning further;
- *Providing Sufficient Opportunities to Learn*: This means they need to encounter new learning and in a variety of different tasks and contexts; and
- *E-learning and Pedagogy*: The use of ICT is intended to provide a learning environment which helps students to make connections with each other, and to facilitate shared learning – for example, by allowing students to create communities outside their classrooms, where they may share resources and provide access to digital resources and virtual experiences.

The Curriculum also forms the basis for assessment (http://assessment.tki.org.nz/), which can involve either Curriculum-based *Achievement Standards*, or competency based *Unit Standards* (https://www.nzqa.govt.nz/ncea/understanding-ncea/how-ncea-works/standards/), both of which are detailed and registered on the *National Qualifications Framework* (https://www.nzqa.govt.nz/studying-in-new-zealand/understand-nz-quals/nzqf/). These Standards are then used to award qualifications in Years 11–13. Qualifications include the *National Certificate of Educational Achievement* (https://www.nzqa.govt.nz/ncea/), and other national and international certificates schools may choose to offer, such as the International Baccalaureate.

Based on the New Zealand Curriculum, and Science Curriculum, in our research that we used as the learning context for LEOS, we identified a number of Achievement Standards which we felt would be suited to, and benefit from, the use of LEOS.

The first standard was AS90943: *The Design Game: Keeping Your Home Warm*, a standard which belonged to the *Physical World* strand. According to the curriculum: "This strand provides explanation for a wide range of physical phenomena, including light, sound, heat, electricity, wave, forces, motion and energy. By studying this strand, students will gain understanding of interactions between parts of the physical world, understand a wide range of contemporary issues and challenges and potential technological problems" (MoE, 2007, p. 45).

The second standard explored was AS90926: *A Biological Issue, Protecting Biodiversity*, which belonged to the *Living World* strand (MoE, 2007). This strand focused on living things, and how they interact with each other and the environment. Here, "students are expected to develop an understanding of the diversity of life, life processes, and the impact of humans on other forms of life. As a result, it is intended they will be able to make decisions about significant biological issues, such as the sustainability of New Zealand's unique flora and fauna and its distinctive fragile ecosystems" (MoE, 2007, p. 45).

The third standard studied was AS90954: *Astronomical Cycle and its Effects on Planet Earth*, a standard which belonged to the *Planet Earth and Beyond* strand (MoE, 2007). This strand is about linking the astronomical cycles such as spin of the Earth, orbit of the Earth around the Sun, and the orbit of the Moon around the Earth, and their effects on planet Earth. Students are expected to "develop an understanding of how the movement of the three celestial bodies impact on the weather, phases of the Moon, tidal movement and in creating solar and lunar eclipses. As a result, it is intended that students will be able to appreciate interconnecting systems and processes on the Earth, the other parts of the Solar System, and the Universe beyond" (MoE, 2007, p. 45).

The fourth standard studied was AS90931: *Demonstrate Understanding of the Chemistry in a Technological Application*, a standard which belonged to the *Chemical World* (Ministry of Education, 2007). The standard focused on students studying about a technological application and the use of Chemistry to meet the needs of society. As a result of completing this standard, the students should be able to appreciate how chemical principles are linked to materials used such as detergents, cement, food and beverages, cosmetics and pharmaceuticals.

INDEX

B
behaviorism, 11–13

C
constructivism, 11–14
    personal, 12, 13
    social, 9, 11, 12, 14, 16, 20

D
didactic, 17, 18, 20, 28, 44
Digitally-Integrated Fieldtrip Inventory (DIFI), 43, 47–53
    cognitive component, 43, 49, 52
    procedural component, 47–48, 52
    social component, 48–49, 52
distributed cognition, 15

E
enviro-school, 25

F
field-based experiences/fieldtrips, ix, 4, 5, 7, 9, 25, 27, 31, 34–41, 50, 53, 63, 65, 74, 76, 89, 102, 104

I
Informal Science Institution (ISI), 4, 5, 9, 17, 34

L
learning, ix, 3–23, 25–31, 33–35, 37–40, 43–52, 57, 61, 65, 67, 74, 76, 79, 81, 92, 93, 95, 102, 104, 105, 107, 108
    active, 7, 8, 20, 30, 31, 33, 34, 44, 45, 47,
    environment, 4, 7, 9, 10, 14, 16, 17, 22, 25, 29–31, 38, 44–46, 49, 50, 92, 108
    formal, 3–5, 8, 9, 11, 15, 17–20, 22, 23, 25, 29–31, 33, 43, 44, 47, 50, 52
    free choice, 3, 5, 8, 10, 19, 21, 25, 34, 37, 38, 40, 49, 52
    integrated, 6, 7, 28, 33, 43, 107
    non-formal, 3–5, 8, 10, 11, 17–23, 25, 30, 31, 33, 43, 47, 52
    self-directed, 21, 31, 34, 44
Learning in Science Project (LISP), 13
Learner-Integrated Field Trip Inventory (LIFTI), 33–35, 43, 47
    cognitive component, 33, 34, 39, 40
    procedural component, 34–36
    social component, 34, 37–39
Learning Management System (LMS), 3, 5–7, 9, 45

M
mediated action, 15, 16
moodle, 5, 7, 9, 43, 45, 48, 49, 61, 62, 65, 71, 73, 76, 77, 85, 87, 99, 101, 104, 106

P
paradigm, 11
    interpretive, 13
    scientific/positivist, 12
psychological tools, 16

S
situated activity, 15
sociocultural theories of learning, 11, 12, 14–17
social affordances, 45, 46

T
theories of learning, 11, 13, 23
transactional distance, 6, 45, 46, 52